ROCK
FURTHER PROOF OF GOD'S SENSE OF HUMOR

ROCK

FURTHER PROOF OF GOD'S SENSE OF HUMOR

C. B. SKELTON, MD

ReadersMagnet, LLC

ROCK, Further Proof of God's Sense of Humor
Copyright © 2018 by C. B. Skelton, MD

Published in the United States of America
ISBN Paperback: 978-1-948864-02-2
ISBN Hardback: 978-1-948864-87-9
ISBN eBook: 978-1-948864-03-9

All rights reserved. No part of this publication may be reproduced, stored in a retrieval system or transmitted in any way by any means, electronic, mechanical, photocopy, recording or otherwise without the prior permission of the author except as provided by USA copyright law.

The opinions expressed by the author are not necessarily those of ReadersMagnet, LLC.

ReadersMagnet, LLC
10620 Treena Street, Suite 230 | San Diego, California, 92131 USA
1.619. 354. 2643 | www.readersmagnet.com

Book design copyright © 2018 by ReadersMagnet, LLC. All rights reserved.
Cover design by Ericka Walker
Interior design by Shieldon Watson

DEDICATION

THIS BOOK IS DEDICATED to my nephew, Willis Newton Moore, BA., J. D., Ph. D., whom I love and admire as if he were my own son. This is despite the fact that he has served for many years as a plaintiff's attorney. However, he always refused frivolous lawsuits against physicians and only pursued those in which the patient suffered serious harm due to true medical malpractice or malfunction of medical equipment.

Newton was a true unsung hero of the Vietnam War where he served as an infantry sergeant in the Marine Corps. Some of his Marine Corps buddies referred to him as "that sergeant we'd follow anywhere." His Vietnam career ended when he was wounded and medevaced on a mission for which he volunteered even though he was scheduled to be sent home. He received no Purple Heart or any other recognition for this injury.

As an attorney, his alma mater, Mercer University thought enough of him to select him as their first in-house general counsel immediately upon his graduation in 1975. As a trial lawyer, he has the respect of his peers because of his thorough preparation for and convincing presentation of his client's case. He has the respect of judges in the courts where he has tried a case. He certainly has the respect of this author because of his persistence to succeed despite many adverse conditions in his earlier life, and also his love for and loyalty to me.

Being human, he is not perfect, but he is still a person one would do well to "follow anywhere."

C. B. Skelton, MD

CONTENTS

Rock, a Big Baby 9
Finances Head for the Rocks 17
The Rock Starts To Roll 21
Learning Hard-Rock Basics 27
Decisions Rock the Boat 41
Growing Up Is Hard as a Rock 57
A Rolling Rock Gathers No Moss 77
A Rock-Solid Soldier 101
A Group of Rockheads 117
LTC. K. I. Kilts, Chief Rockhead 123
Rock-Bottom in Commanders 141
The Rock Still Rolls 161
One More Rock to Climb 193
The Rock Rolls through Med School 211

Epilogue 225

ROCK, A BIG BABY

"Push, Rosa, push," Doctor Osborne exhorted in an irritated voice. "Come on, push hard. You ought to know by now how hard you have to push. This ain't your first baby. It's your tenth one, ain't it?"

Rosa shook her head in violent denial. "That's not true," she objected, as huge tears cascaded down each of her ruddy, high cheeks that were normally wreathed in bright smiles. Those high cheekbones and her dark hair were the only physical hints of the strong Indian heritage she proudly claimed. She could not present absolute proof to support it, but she always contended that someone had traced her family lineage back to Pocahontas, her great-great-great-great grandmother.

"You're right," continued Dr. Osborne, "You told me that before, but I had done forgot. Those five oldest ones ain't yores. Yore old man had done had them before he married you, hadn't he?

"My God, why in the world would a young girl like you do something dumb like that? Looks to me like even a fool would have more sense than to marry a guy who already had five younguns and then go and have a batch of her own. That guy must really have a gift for gab to talk an intelligent and pretty girl like you into something that foolhardy. I sure do wish God had 'a given me a line like he obviously has. Ain't no telling where I could'a been right now if I could sweet talk that-a-way.

"Come on, Rosa, push hard. We're gonna be here all night the way you're doin' right now. You were so good and did just what I told you the last time you had a baby, and we got that one over with and done in a hurry. Now you act as if you ain't never done anything like this before. I just don't understand it."

Doc Osborne was a crusty old general practitioner of medicine who had worked in the Atlanta area for many years. Nobody seemed to know what medical school he had attended or even if he had attended one. In those days, a person could contract themselves out to study medicine under the tutelage of a licensed physician for a certain period of years. Then, if he could pass the examination given by the Georgia Board of Medical Examiners, he could hang out his shingle to practice medicine anywhere in the State of Georgia. Perhaps that is what Doc had done. It didn't matter one bit to Rosa. He was her doctor and she trusted him implicitly.

"Doc Osborne has a license to practice Medicine in Georgia, and he always seems to get the job done quite well in spite of the fact that he drinks a little too much toddy at times," she reasoned. Nor did Rosa like the fact that Doc had such poor usage of the English language. She had very little formal education and had worked so hard to learn the correct word usages. Even though she hated those aspects of her doctor's life and character, they had nothing to do with his medical knowledge and ability. Furthermore, other doctors respected his abilities enough that some of them called him in consultation on occasion. Those considerations seemed good enough for her to accept him as her physician despite his obvious shortcomings.

"Nobody is perfect," she would say when she heard her doctor criticized.

Rosa had recently turned 26 and this child would be her fifth in less than seven years of marriage to Newton. Every one of those children had been born at home, and Doc Osborne had delivered the previous four. Most of the time, he had been paid in full for the last delivery before the next delivery came due…a difficult achievement for working-class couples of those days, especially in the poverty stricken State of Georgia.

From all appearances, Doc was financially successful in his medical practice and he could hardly wait for the new 1927 T-Model Fords to come off of the assembly lines. He had one of those mechanical marvels on order because the unpaved roads around Atlanta and the big potholes that were so prevalent in the paved ones had already "shaken the innards" out of his old '25 model-T. This purchase contract meant he needed to have 650 cash dollars on hand to pay for his new vehicle by no later than December first and here it was nearly the middle of August. Doc Osborne had plenty of cause to hurry.

"Why don't you push like you did when you had all those other babies, Rosa?" plead the impatient medic. "You act as if you think this baby weighs a ton. Well, I'll make you a guarantee, he doesn't. I'll bet I've weighed a heap of catfish on my scales that were heavier than he'll be if you ever, for God's sake, start pushin' an' we get him here.

"Come on, Rosa, push hard and let's get this thing over with… that's the way. Now you're doin' somethin'. Why in the world haven't you pushed like this before?

"My God, look at that head…plumb full of red hair. Anybody else in your family redheaded?

"OK, now, just one more push and I think we'll get this thing over with…atta girl…push hard now…here he comes.

"Oh my Lord, I do believe this' un really is the biggest young'un I have ever delivered, and we did it right here in yore home to a little bitty Mama who ain't much bigger than a toothpick. I wonder if maybe we've set a record of some kind?

"Holy moley, just look at the size of this big ol' young man. I'll tell you one thing: he's gonna give any catfish I ever weighed on my scales quite a run for his money, if he don't maybe even beat him.

"Wow, just look at how he pulls them scales down nearly to the bottom. Thirteen pounds and ten ounces…there ain't no question about it. He is the biggest baby I ever weighed on these scales—but I did weigh one catfish that went just a little bit over 17 pounds.

"Can you believe it? Little-bitty Rosa has the biggest baby I ever delivered in my whole life and him redheaded at that…and we done it at home.

"Uh-oh, what's this?…Oh, it's only a natural circumcision. It sure ain't never gonna cause him no problems. Don't you worry about it none, Rosa.

"Man, that's really somethin'. Not only is he the biggest baby I ever delivered, but he's the first one I ever seen who had a natural circumcision. I can't wait to see Dr. Bertram to find if he ever seen anything like this."

By this time, Rosa had dried her tears. Now she looked at Dr. Osborne with near panic in her eyes as she fairly shouted, "Doc, don't you try to hide anything from me. Tell me the truth. What's wrong with my baby?"

"Aw, honey, quit your worryin'," replied the doctor, "it ain't nothin' but a little ol' natural circumcision. In them big medical terms, it's a little ol' abnormality us doctors call hypospadias. It's one of them conditions where the pee-hole is on the underside of his little thing-a-ma-bob instead of bein' in the center at the very tip of it, like most of 'em are. They explained to me when I was studying what they call Embryology back when I was in school, that when a baby boy is being formed in his mama's womb, his little thing-a-ma-bob starts off as a plumb flat blob—like rolled-out biscuit dough or something like that. Normally, it rolls itself into a little round weenie-looking thing and it leaves the middle open to make the pee-tube on the inside of it.

"This' un just didn't completely roll up quite all the way out to the end, and it leaves a sort of slit on the underside. That means the foreskin don't quite go plumb around the tip of his little tally-whacker and it's easy to roll back so there ain't no way it can get tight and hang up like others sometimes do. Maybe now, you can understand why some folks call it a natural circumcision.

"Now, I'm gonna tell you the real reason you don't need to worry. Unless the pee-hole is way far back from the tip of his little thing—back towards the middle of the shaft—it don't mean nothing…and this' un shore ain't far back.

"Just don't you worry none, Honey. When it comes the proper time, he'll be able to make you grandma just like any other young man. In the meantime, with that teeny little-bitty opening he's gonna have to pee through, he'll be able to pee further and higher than any other boy in the whole state of Georgia. That should make all the other boys jealous. Yep, he should be the grand champeen long distance pee-er of the whole State of Georgia. I'll bet he won't have no peers among all of them other little pee-ers."

Doc could not refrain from laughing at his own play on words. "Man, that shore is a good 'un," he said. "No peers among little pee-ers. I'll have to be sure to remember that'un so I can tell all of them fellows down at the lodge…

"And, Rosa, you and your husband had just better be real thankful 'cause I won't be having to make you no charge for a circumcision. That'll save you somewhere in the neighborhood of 'bout three dollars.

"By the way, from looking at this here placenta, it looks like there might' a been another little cord comin' off from it close to the outer edge right here, and there's this little knot-like thing hooked to it. It looks to me as if it just might have been another baby at one time, but it shore is dried up now.

"My God, can you imagine little ol' you havin' twins with one of 'em weighing nearly 14 pounds. That'd be one for the history books and it mighta' even made me famous—but it didn't happen that' a way. Just my luck. I guess this big fellow you got here just completely starved the other'un out. He shore does look like he might'a been eatin' for two.

"OK now, Rosa," continued Dr. Osborne "That's enough of this silly small talk. We've gotta have a name for this big ol' redhead, and our Governor's new law says we've gotta do it right away or they'll prosecute me. Seems to me it's gettin to be sorta' like it was back in the days of Moses when them Egyptians were scared the Jewish people might have too many babies and they wanted to control the number of 'em.

"I don't know what this country's coming to the way the government is gettin' involved in everything. You can't even have a baby without them politicians stickin' their noses right into yore bedroom and wantin' to know everything about it…What time was he born? How much did he weigh? How many other kids in the family? How old is his Mama and his Papa? Why is that any of their business?

"What difference does it make to the government what time of the day he was born at or how old is his Mama and Papa? Pretty soon, you won't even be able to even go to the outhouse without askin' their permission."

Then Doc turned to Rosa and said, "Now tell me, what do you want to name this big ol' young'un?"

"We thought if he was a boy, we'd name him Selrach, after my Daddy," she answered. "I suppose I just like that name because it is Daddy's name, but we plan to call him 'Rock.' Don't you think that will be a cute nickname?"

Doc Osborne gave no answer.

"His middle name is Tynarb," Rosa continued. Mr. Tynarb Nutshell is a fine Christian gentleman who has been good to my family, especially when Newton was sick for such a long time. You know him. He's the one who runs Nutshell's dairy. He told us that as long as he had a bottle of milk, he'd make certain none of our children would ever have to go hungry."

Doc Osborne could not hold his tongue or his laughter one minute longer. His rotund belly shook with each roar like the rolling waves in the ocean. "Lord have mercy, what will the neighbors think? Rosa has a youngun that comes here redheaded and half-grown, and then she names him after the milkman. Man, that's a good 'un. I can't wait 'til our next meeting so I can report that 'un to the boys down at the lodge. But I promise you honey, I won't use your name."

Large, redheaded and with a seemingly meaningless deformity, fate threw the infant Rock into the ocean of life. Only the good Lord knew on what course his life would be steered from this time forward. Thank God, a handful of people cared.

FINANCES HEAD FOR THE ROCKS

"Rosa, Rosa, come here quick." Eloise's loud scream reverberated through the entire house from the downstairs bedroom. Her semi-hysterical bellowing gave Rosa a terrible fright. Rock was only a little over two weeks old at the time, and she had left her red headed infant lying naked in the middle of the bed alongside Eloise and her newborn son, Jesse Jr., while she ran upstairs to find a clean diaper.

Rosa had not allowed herself the ten days of bed-rest Dr. Osborne said were needed after her delivery, but she lovingly supplied that luxury for her sister-in-law, whose baby came ten days after Rock's arrival. Even with the responsibility for their seven children living at home, Rosa felt it her solemn duty to care for her brother's wife, who had a reputation of being somewhat weaker than most women. Eloise expected—and made the most of—the kid-glove treatment she received at the hand of her sister-in-law. There were many who thought she took advantage of Rosa's good nature and self-sacrificial service.

As she almost flew down the stairs in response to Eloise's loud outcry, Rosa had clear visions of her latest offspring lying crumpled and injured, or possibly dead on the floor after having fallen from the bed. Instead of finding the terrible tragedy she so greatly feared, her malingering patient greeted her with hysterical laughter.

"Just look up there at that wet ceiling, Rosa," exclaimed the still-laughing Eloise as she pointed to the peeling tongue-and-groove ceiling of the old bedroom. "How tall is the ceiling in this room, anyhow?"

"I really don't know, but I think I heard Newton say that it's something like maybe 12 feet," Rosa answered with a puzzled look on her face. Then she continued, "Why in the world did you call me down here to ask me such a fool question—and what does how tall this ceiling is have to do with your being in such hysterics?"

"Well, just about the time you got to the top of the stairs there, little Rock decided to pee. When he started peeing and he didn't have a diaper on to stop it, that stream of urine hit the ceiling like a water-jet. It splattered all over little Jesse and me, and just about everything else in this bedroom.

"I don't know how high it would have gone if the ceiling hadn't been there, but the way it splattered when it hit, it didn't look like it was slowing down one bit," a still laughing Eloise chortled as she used the bed's top sheet to wipe urine and tears from her face and from her infant son. "I just know I've never seen anything close to being as funny as that in my entire life," she concluded.

As Rosa stared for a moment at the few clear drops of liquid that still hung ominously from the ceiling above Eloise and Jesse, she thought to thank God that the stream of urine had not hit the electrical junction overhead. She knew there were dangerous electrical connections inside that unsealed ceramic box. The electrical cord dangled from it and led to a small light bulb, the only source of light for the room. She had heard tales about young boys being painfully shocked when older boys persuaded them to urinate on the sparkplugs of tractors or T-Model Fords while their motors were idling. That boyish prank, though painful, was not life threatening.

Even with her limited knowledge of electricity, Rosa was aware that the alternating current going through that light cord was far more dangerous than the DC current from a battery or a magneto. She also knew that urine is an excellent conductor of electric current, and the thought frightened her considerably.

"Doc Osborne told us he'd be able to pee a long way, but he didn't tell us it would be a water-cannon," she said to Eloise as she turned to leave the room again to finally retrieve that needed diaper. "I'd better hurry and get something to cover that dangerous weapon before someone gets hurt."

Within his family group, Rock's long-range urinary emissions became a comedic legend, but no one ever dared to speak of the fact outside of the immediate family. It was a tightly held family secret until the time when, at a much later date, Rock used public outhouses or bathrooms without a family attendant. When that time arrived, the redhead would have a boyish tendency to show off his unusual "gift."

When Rock was about two, his younger sister was born, necessitating another visit by Doc Osborne. This time, Rosa's labor was much shorter because the baby was much smaller, and there was not time for prolonged conversation between the two. That suited both Rosa and her beloved Doc quite well.

The financial situation at that time was much better for Newton and Rosa and they were able to pay Doc's fee in cold cash. Because of the improved financial condition, they had already made a down payment on an existing home and had moved into their new dwelling. Their credit record was absolutely impeccable and Newton, wanting to share his good fortune, was considering cosigning notes for two of his closest friends to help them purchase homes for their families.

"Oh Newton," Rosa implored, "I just wish you wouldn't sign those notes with Grady and Randall. If they should forfeit on them, we would never be able to pay their notes and our house payments, too. We might lose everything."

"But, Rosa, they are both such fine Christian men and are just having a hard time raising enough cash for a down payment. I believe they deserve some help, and that it is our Christian duty to give it to them," Newton retorted. "Both of these men are much too dependable to ever go bankrupt and leave their indebtedness to us. Besides, if the shoe were on the other foot, they would do the same thing for us. Honey, you just worry too much," said Newton as he headed for the bank to co sign the notes.

"Remember the Bible says not to be surety for anyone," Rosa blurted as she slammed the door behind her stubborn husband.

THE ROCK STARTS TO ROLL

The great depression struck unexpectedly and in all its fury shortly after Rock had celebrated his third birthday. Just as Rosa had feared, both Grady and Randall filed for bankruptcy, leaving their indebtedness for Newton to pay. Each of them made a tearful apology to their friend and co-signer and suggested that he file for bankruptcy protection, also.

Newton refused to follow what he called "that cowardly path of bankruptcy." Instead, he insisted, "Our good name is worth much more to my family and me than anybody's thousand dollars. With God's help and our hard work, we will pay every dime we owe."

No one in the family had any idea how difficult that course of action would be or how long it would take to repay the indebtedness. That decision indelibly staked out the tortuous and torturing course the family's financial path would take for many years to come.

When the bank foreclosed on their recently purchased home in Atlanta a few months later, Newton and Rosa moved their family into a three-room, rented, rundown shack near Riverdale, Georgia. As the ancient Model-T Ford truck chugged and rattled southward down the unpaved highway 41, leaving the city of Atlanta in its smoking wake, it carried all the family's remaining meager possessions.

At first, Rock thought of it as a wonderful treat to sit up front with the big boys in the old truck's open cab; but when the bone-chilling wind of that November night came whipping over the windshield, it sent him scurrying to the floorboard for cover. Crouched in the floor of the truck's cab, he tried to roll himself into a ball like an opossum to keep warm. He huddled as closely as he possibly could to the vent of the old-fashioned manifold heater, and relished the precious warmth that poured from its opening.

When the boy woke up early on the first morning inside his pitifully substandard new residence and peeled back his heavy covering of homemade quilts, he was quite excited. He thought it was neat to be able to look through the cracks between the boards in the floor and see the family's chickens. He also thought it was fun to see the rays of sun that cascaded through the nail holes in the house's metal roof, highlighting the specks of dust swirling in the air. At the time, however, he gave no thought to the fact that the chickens under the house and the dust had any connection. He never did learn a proper appreciation for the merciless torrents of cold wind that incessantly poured through those same cracks in the wintertime, bringing a tooth-chattering chill in their wake.

In their new, quite rural location, the family became tenant farmers, which is socially only a small step above being sharecroppers. The major difference between the two classes of workers is that a sharecropper has no investment in the crop or the operation of the farm other than the labor he and his family provide. No matter how meager the crop happens to be, he is certain he will get his assigned percentage of that yield as the wage for his labor.

On the other hand, a tenant farmer rents the land from its owner, usually on an annual basis, for a stated amount of money. The tenant must then furnish everything needed to perform the complete farming operation: tools, livestock, fertilizer and such. In addition to that, he must do, or hire done, all of the labor needed to produce the crop. In many cases, the tenant farmer's expenses to produce the crop exceed his income from its sale, but the rent remains fixed and comes due regardless of whether or not a farmer has any profit from his farming operation. When that happens, the tenant farmer's outcome becomes even more pitiable than that of the poorest sharecropper.

Life on the farm proved to be exceedingly hard for the family. The work of clearing the new ground needed for their farming operation proved to be slow and tedious, back-breaking labor that certainly did not produce an income. Especially during those deepest depression times, conveniences were very few or absent, and the thought of any comforts was merely a pipe dream for a tenant farmer.

Rock soon learned the real reason for his family's insistence on having a copy of the current Sears and Roebuck catalog in the little shack at the end of the path behind the house, even though there never seemed to be enough money available to order any of the catalog's merchandise. The book came in quite handy for both reading and learning about the modern day clothing and equipment, but it had another, even more vital use.

One could greatly enhance the third use for the catalog if he simply tore a page out of the huge book and rolled the torn-out page into a very tight ball. He must then unroll the paper ball before putting the paper to this very practical use. This procedure made the paper feel softer and made it work much more effectively, because the crumpling action did away with the slippery, slick sheen and texture of the paper. A slick surface does not clean well, as witness the rough texture of the modern washcloth. Pages from the wish-book were a huge improvement over corncobs, the alternative type of material available for use in the cleaning needed in outdoor facilities of this type.

Everyone in the farming community lived by the constant code that nothing should be wasted…even corncobs. They were quite plentiful during most of the year and were available in two natural colors, red and white. For some reason, the red corncobs greatly outnumbered the white ones in his family's supply, so Rock was taught in an early outdoor lesson to use three red cobs, and then to use a white one to see if he needed to use more red ones. It was certainly a crude and cruel comedown from toilet tissue, but corncobs were certainly not smooth or slick, and were therefore quite effective.

With the advent of the depression and the death of his beloved Grampa Turner, the thing that bothered the boy even more than having rare or nonexistent conveniences was that his supply of precious pennies had totally dried up. He could no longer purchase any treats such as stick candy, suckers, soft drinks, chewing gum and the like.

His parents were too proud to allow Rock to beg for or even hint for—and they certainly forbad him to steal—those small sweet candy or cookie treasures for which his heart (not to mention his stomach) so often longed. They had been so easy to get when Grampa Turner was living.

However, there did exist an occasional opportunity to earn a small number of the items he so strongly desired. Out of sheer necessity, and shamelessly hoping his audience would recompense him for his performance, the four-year-old made up (he could not write) his first composition. He performed his simple song with a simple tune for customers in Riverdale's small general store, Munday's Store, any time he was there with his parents and given half a chance.

> Rocky, he's a good little boy.
> Rocky, he's a dandy.
> Rocky, he's a good little boy
> and he likes striped-candy.

Occasionally, someone might reward the boy's efforts with a penny or two, which he would immediately exchange with Mr. Munday for the sweet object of his heart's desire. Most of the time, however, the people in his audience were equally as poverty stricken as was the young redhead, and could not spare him even one red cent for his entertainment efforts.

By this time, Rock had gained enough experience with abject poverty that he could have proper empathy with their situation. He had developed a complete and total understanding of what it meant to be poor.

LEARNING HARD-ROCK BASICS

Especially during the depression years, an extremely high percentage of the rural south population depended on farming for their livelihood. Families were generally quite large because they needed every possible worker for planting their crops in the spring and gathering the harvest in the fall. Most families were forced to consider the education of their children a distant second compared to producing a crop, because their survival depended on the yield from their fields at harvest time.

For this reason, the community usually began the fall school sessions after the crops had been gathered and safely stored. Classes would continue throughout the winter months until the planting season was in swing again in the early spring. During the entire school year, the days were relatively short and, conversely, the nights were long. After-school chores took up most, if not all, of the after-school daylight hour when the days were so short. This meant that a student had to study at night.

In Rock's family, every family member beginning at age four had his or her assigned chore to be done on a daily basis. Rock's duty was to keep the wood-box beside the cook-stove filled with stove-wood that the older boys had cut. When his father assigned this duty to the boy he challenged him, "Son, there must always be enough wood kept in the box so your Mother will have fuel for cooking our meals. This is an extremely important job, and our entire family is depending on you. You know we cannot live and work without food, and your mother cannot cook without wood. We are depending on you to do your job well."

The redhead's chest swelled with pride as his father entrusted him with such great responsibility, and he made a solemn promise to his father, "Yessir, Daddy. I will do my very best."

Although it seemed a never-ending task to him, he liked his job. He got to be near the cooking where he could taste the food, which "helped" his mother with the seasoning. He also was allowed to lick the pans where goodies had been prepared, and he could stay near the warm stove most of the time when it was so cold.

In the days before rural electrification, the only source of light for night time activity for virtually all rural southern households was the kerosene lamp. The family usually placed a lighted lamp on a table in the middle of the room, or secured it in a lamp-holder attached to the wall at or above eye-level.

The sparseness of lighted areas in their home forced the family to become a more closely-knit unit, because they had to gather around the flickering lamplight. Radio was in its infancy and was only available to the more affluent rural households. TV existed only in the remote corners of daydreaming inventor's minds. Therefore, reading, singing, game-playing and chatty talk or playful nagging were the major items of family entertainment.

Rock's family had managed to keep the old upright piano when they suffered their great depression losses, and it became their gathering point and source of entertainment after supper each night. Newton had received two piano lessons in his youth, and could play many songs acceptably for his family to harmonize. All frustration about any problems seemed to be lost in these sessions.

As his family turned to reading and study each night, the clumsy, hyperactive redhead wiggled and wandered about among the older children as an equal opportunity tormenter. He attentively looked over the shoulders of his older siblings, or he sat in their laps or sprawled out on the floor beside them as they read their books and prepared their lessons. In a short time, he knew every word in each of the Baby Ray books his older sisters were poring over as they did their reading assignments for the first and second grades. He had also learned to say the alphabet in its entirety and he could solve most of the first and second-grade math problems. His proud mother secured an audience for her son with the Superintendent of Clayton County Schools, and Rock demonstrated his skills before that official. Because there was no kindergarten in the school system, the school superintendent gave his permission for Rosa to enroll the boy in the first grade although he had barely reached the age of five.

The first and second grades met in the same classroom at Riverdale School, with Miss Corey as teacher. Rock quickly became a favorite with her, and why shouldn't he? He already knew his ABC's, could count well past 100, and could already read every page of Baby Ray. The boy appeared to be an ideal student, with the exception of his handwriting, which was horrendous. After Miss Corey finally learned to decipher the scribbled writing in his homework, Rock required almost no extra work at all on her part. She rewarded him with an A+ in Reading, Math, and Conduct, and even fudged enough to give him a B+ in Writing, "...Because he tries so hard. Rock is a pleasure to teach," she scrawled as her comment on his first report card.

While Rock fared quite well in the academic medium of the schoolroom, the athletic part of schoolyard play was altogether a different matter. Despite the fact that he was physically as large as most of the boys and girls in his class, he was a year or two behind every one of them in emotional and physiological maturity. In addition, being redheaded and freckle-faced made him appear different from the other kids and opened him up to be the victim of much teasing and many taunts.

Rock hated it when one of his classmates and supposed friends would heckle him with, "I'd rather be dead than red on the head." If the redhead showed any reaction (which he usually did) another boy would join in the taunting with a remark like, "Tell me ol' Freckle Face. What happened? Did you swallow a ten dollar bill and it break out in pennies?"

Early in his school life, Rock learned that the old adage, *sticks and stones may break my bones, but words can never harm me*, is a total lie. Day after day, he heard the same degrading taunts, and every one of them hurt him deep inside. When he reacted to defend himself, the heckler easily outran him or, worse still, the heckler stood his ground and the boy got a good dose of old-fashioned knuckle-stew.

There seemed to be no way he could win in this arena where he was physically and emotionally the least mature of all the kids in the class. For this reason, Rock reacted to school in a manner that was exactly the opposite of most children's reactions: he loved the classroom, where he was excelling and learning something new every day, but he hated recess time with its endless confrontations.

Just before Thanksgiving of his first year in school, he heard what he thought was wonderful news. The family was moving to another rented farm in Jonesboro. "Hooray," exulted the redhead. "Now I won't have to put up with all of these bullies any more."

The family quickly adjusted to the move to Jonesboro, but all of the ingredients for unhappiness for the boy were still there—or possibly, they were even greater. Rock was still the youngest and least mature student in his classroom. He was still redheaded and freckle-faced. All that had really changed was his location; and, to make matters worse, now he was the new kid in school.

His new teacher, Miss Dixon, was younger and much prettier than Miss Corey, but she was more insightful and a lot tougher. She almost immediately saw through the boy's facade of being able to read Baby Ray so perfectly. She discerned that he had committed every page in the book to memory, and could recite it word-for-word just by recognizing the picture on the page. Miss Dixon would turn to different pages in the book and point out individual words. "What is that word, Rock?" she would ask the surprised boy.

Rock could come up with the word eventually, but only after he had recognized the picture on the page and had mentally gone through every memorized word that preceded her pointing finger. The charade was finished. This robbed him of his academic superiority, his greatest point of pride. For the first time in his short lifetime, even he clearly realized he could not read. Now, the boy felt totally convinced that he was the lowest of the low.

In all of his time in school at Riverdale and at Jonesboro, the redhead had never been able to hold his own in athletic contests or pugilistic encounters with classmates because of his physical immaturity. Now he had great fear that he could not even hold his own in reading. He knew of only one area where he was far, far superior to all the other boys in the school but, because of its delicate nature, he did not have the freedom to reveal it or to use it to an advantage.

There was no opportunity for him to dazzle other boys in the Jonesboro school with his spectacular talent in the little, dark, outdoor, community toilet with four holes that Clayton County had provided for boys. Furthermore, he knew that a true gentleman would not under any circumstance ever even try to show a girl how far he could pee. Therefore, his feeling of frustration mounted.

Rock knew that he lagged far behind his first-grade classmates in his reading skills, and Miss Dixon did not have time to offer him individual instruction in that subject. She had already gone over that material with the whole class before the redhead arrived in Jonesboro. It was up to him and his family, now, if the boy should ever learn to read.

Every day, he hurried home after school and retreated to his special domain, the stove-wood box. Here he would lie on top of the freshly-cut stove-wood and enjoy its clean pine smell as, night after night, he wrestled with individual words in Baby Ray. He was trying to recognize a pattern in them and possibly break their elusive code. In Rock's boyish mind, the period of time he struggled with his reading seemed interminable before the determined lad suddenly leapt from the wood-box one evening. With a shout of joy, he exulted, "Oh, Mother, I can read. I can read. It came to me just like a window-shade rolling up."

From that moment on, he stood able to compete on an equal basis with any child on his grade level in any general subject. The embattled boy's actions soon began to show evidence that he had regained a slight degree of self-respect.

Cotton reigned as king in Dixie during those depression days. It had long held the reputation of being the best money crop anyone could plant. Thankfully, Rock's father had his rented farm planted in that pest-infested weed for only one summer. It happened the summer after the boy had completed the second grade.

Being barely seven, Rock had no responsibilities in the cultivation of their cotton crop except to do a little chopping, but he was too young to decide which plants to sacrifice. He felt grown-up that fall as he set out for his first venture at cotton picking. He proudly hooked over his shoulder the strap of his personal burlap cotton-picking bag his mother had made for him, and headed to the cotton field with visions of picking more cotton than anyone had ever picked before.

Only those who have personally labored in the fields at cotton-picking time can have full empathy with the boy's problems during those sweltering hot days. Even at age seven, back pain drove the boy to his knees. He had to crawl and reach upward to remove lint from cotton bolls hanging from stalks that sometimes towered over his head even when he was standing. Rock's back pain was far exceeded at weigh-in time by the painful fact that his entire day's work produced just over 25 pounds of cotton while his older sister, little Rosa, averaged about 150 pounds a day. He had been soundly beaten by a girl.

"Rock, you just ain't no cotton-pickin' cotton picker," little Rosa repeatedly ridiculed him as she received adulations from other family members for her prowess.

His first (and only) season in the cotton field brought more than considerable pain and embarrassment to the redhead in an unusual way. It also brought great fear for the safety of his brother, James.

A local citizen in Jonesboro began to call a fellow worker by the unwanted nickname of "Oh Boy." The man hated the appellation so much that he took his coworker to court where he requested a restraining order against his being called by that name. The judge granted his request. To the great dismay of most citizens in the community, not only did the judge's order restrain his co worker, but it also extended to all citizens of the county. The case was the meat of local gossip for a number of months.

At the same time, one of the more popular local bakeries marketed its product under the trade name of Oh Boy Bread. James seemed to take great pleasure in repeatedly yelling at the top of his lungs, "Oh Boy" and then almost inaudibly saying, "Bread." Rock could clearly envision the sheriff with a posse of deputies swooping down on the cotton field every time he heard that yell, and he lived in fear for his hero.

There seemed to be no way that cotton picking season could end quickly enough to suit one hurting, embarrassed, frightened, just-turned-seven-year-old boy. He stood dead on ready to move to another phase of his life.

Doing the family wash was a daunting task that normally took all the females in the family at least an entire day to complete. The site chosen for washing was always located near a spring or well that served as the source for water. They separated the clothes according to color and fabric and placed them in a huge, water-filled, black wash-pot sitting over an open, outdoor, wood fire. Homemade lye soap or, occasionally, commercial Octagon soap was added and the clothes were brought to a boil. They stirred the clothes throughout this boiling cycle using a clean stick or a home made paddle that the women also used to batter any stain spots from the clothes.

The women then used boiling water for rinsing, and all of the clothes went through at least two rinsings. Some garments, also went through a bath of starch solution before the women hung them on an outdoor clothesline to dry. After this, they ironed the clothes with a heavy flatiron heated in the fireplace or on the cook-stove.

The redhead was in the third grade when an illness forced his father to miss work for several months. The financial plight of the family became desperate, and his parents made a decision that his mother had to become the temporary breadwinner for the family in a time when few women worked outside the home.

Grandma Turner, Rosa's mother, had taken Rosa out of school before she completed the second grade and, therefore, she had few educational qualifications for any job. Her mother believed strongly in education—but only for boys. She had told her daughter, "The only jobs girls ever do are to keep house and raise babies. You surely do not need any kind of education for that. You have learned how to read and write. That's enough knowledge for you, young lady. Now, if you want to learn more, go to the library or find yourself a job in a book store."

As soon as she turned twelve, Rosa did find a job at Miller's Book Store in Atlanta. She cleaned floors, stocked the bookshelves, wrapped packages and even waited on customers in an emergency. Best of all, she ravenously read those beloved books at every opportunity. She hungrily devoured every page and applied them to her own life. Because she had such dedication to her study, her lack of formal education in the past was not suspected among any of her present associates.

The family's financial situation became so dire, they killed their last beef, and Rosa began to peddle the meat from door-todoor in an effort to raise money. As fate would have it, one of the doors Rosa knocked on was that of Mrs. Mildred Thompson, an old friend with whom she had lost contact. The two had previously worked together in PTA in DeKalb County, where Rosa served as president. Mrs. Thompson had recently become head of the newly formed US Federal Relief Agency for Clayton County. She suggested that Rosa apply for a position as caseworker, a job her department had not been able to fill. The job specifications in this case called for a person with a college degree. Rosa landed the job despite her lack of formal education in what the family thought was a miracle from God.

Her new employment sometimes made it temporarily impossible for Rosa to do the family's laundry at home. Even though she thought their prices were outrageous, she infrequently had to take the clothes to a commercial laundry in Atlanta. On one of these occasions, Rosa and Newton picked up the clean garments and left them in the open family touring car while they bought a few needed items at the grocery store. Someone absconded with the freshly done laundry. With the exception of the garments that were on his back at the time of the theft, all of Rock's clothes were included in the stolen laundry.

It's bad about my clothes, Rock thought as he dropped off to sleep that night, *but I sure am glad I won't have to go to school tomorrow.*

The next morning, his mother said, "Young man, you know I believe that cleanliness is next to godliness, and those clothes of yours are absolutely too filthy for you to wear to school today." Rock tried to hide his grin of relief upon hearing those wonderful words. "However," his mother continued, "your education is much too important for us to let a little thing like what clothes you wear stand in its way."

At this point, she pulled a homemade flower sack dress that belonged to his sister, Helen, over the boy's head and sent him packing to school. The boy completed the rest of his stay in the Jonesboro Grammar School bearing the added stigma of that one day when he wore a dress to school.

Crops were very poor that year. Only one year of planting cotton had made the soil on that farm so poor it would require too much expensive fertilizer for the family to have any hope for profit if they remained in that location. Therefore, they decided to move to a new location in Mountain View, where they planned to grow mostly fresh vegetables. The older boys would once again clear a large area of new-ground for their farming efforts. No one had tilled the new-ground soil in recent years, and it would be far more fertile and require less fertilizer. That would reduce the cost of raising crops considerably. Furthermore, Mountain View was close to Atlanta, where they would find the best markets to sell their produce.

Rock was nearly eight years old when his family made their move to their new location. Candler Field (destined to later become the Atlanta airport) lay nearby—only a couple of miles away from their farm. He thrilled beyond measure with both the audio and visual proofs of the airfield's closeness. He thought it was exciting to hear the occasional roar of an airplane engine overhead and then to race outside and wave at the pilot of the open-cockpit plane. Once in a while, a pilot would wiggle his wings in reply, or he might possibly even return the children's waves from his lofty position.

The boy did have some remorse about leaving Anne Wooten in Jonesboro. He had just begun to take a little notice of girls and, although he admired her long, blonde, Shirley Temple curls so much, Rock had never gotten enough nerve to tell Anne of his affection…that is except for the one valentine he made with his own hands especially for her.

In Mountain View, Rock established his first enduring friendship with another boy who was not kin to him. Bud Johnson stood about half-a-head taller than the boy, and a little more than two years older. His classmates generally recognized Bud as the strongest and fastest boy in the fourth grade. Of course, Bud first had to establish who was boss of this fourth grade duo, but that was an easy task against the younger competitor. Rock quickly submitted to superior strength and hollered, "calf rope."

With that matter decided, Bud, took the young newcomer under his protective wings against all comers. There may have been an ulterior motive for his friendship, since Bud constantly sought Rock's help with his homework. One day as the two boys played on a terraced hillside in the family watermelon patch, Rock said to Bud, "You can run faster than I can, you can beat me in marbles and baseball or in a fight, and you're stronger than I am. But there's one way I'll bet you can never beat me."

"Yeah," Bud quickly retorted, trying to sound tough, "in what way is that? You just try me, and we'll see."

"I-I-I'll bet I can pee further than you can," Rock hesitantly continued his challenge.

"Well, we'll just see about that," said Bud as he directed his stream of urine onto a targeted plant eight or ten feet away. Let's see you beat that."

Rock's big moment had finally arrived. He took his place on the terrace bank beside Bud and proceeded to clear the next terrace bank nearly 60 feet away with his own stream.

"Gollee-bob," exclaimed Bud, "I ain't never seen nothing like that before."

From that time on, when other boys were present, Bud would show off his protégé by asking Rock to "pee over the outhouse" or "on top of the barn from the ground." These and many other inane acts of urination, the boy accomplished with ease.

All the boys seemed certainly impressed by the redhead's unheard-of prowess in this aspect of physical functions. They even seemed to show a little more respect for the young newcomer who, for most of his school life, had held himself in terribly low esteem because of his clumsiness, his lack of physical prowess and of athletic ability—not to mention his gluttony.

Doc Osborne had proved to be a prophet. For now, Rock had indeed become "the champeen," who had "no peer among little pee-ers."

The boy was extremely bashful around girls, and tried never to let any of the ones he claimed as his "sweetheart" know where she stood with him. That changed drastically in his fourth grade year when June Dane moved into the Mountain View area. June seemed to be so much different from other girls. She had short dark-blonde hair and laughing gray-green eyes. There was a deep dimple in her chin and lesser dimples in each of her rosy cheeks. She was almost as tall as Rock and, although he could never explain why, it did not seem to bother him that she could out run him most of the time.

Rock thought she was the cutest girl he had ever seen and wanted desperately to be her boyfriend. He tried to carry her books home from school every day. After all, she walked in the same direction as he did, and she had to walk even further to reach her home. She needed some help and it was his duty as a gentleman to provide it.

Rock did every possible thing he could think of to impress June. He chased black snakes and squirrels—he even waded in the creek to catch crayfish or lizards, but she seemed unimpressed. One day as, in his courting frenzy, he was flitting to-and-fro, across-and-back on the path toward home, June hollered, "You had better watch out. The green stuff growing up that tree is poison ivy."

"Shucks," said the redhead, "that stuff don't bother me." He grabbed a handful of leaves from the dangerous vine and briskly rubbed them all over his face, neck and arms in his most manly fashion. Then he looked hopefully for some sign of June's approval.

About ten days later, when he finally returned to school almost cleared of his rash, Rock found that neither his textbook toting, his poison ivy antic nor any of his other attention-getters had really endeared him to June. To his great dismay, there she was flirting with a fifth grader.

As Christmas neared a couple of months later, the boy was very excited about Santa's upcoming visit. "Do you still believe in Santa Claus?" June asked derisively.

"Of course I do," was his immediate reply. At the tender age of eight, even though he was already in the fourth grade, Rock was still a strong believer in the jolly old fellow. When June laughed at him for his continued faith in the fat man with whiskers and red suit, Rock became angry. His heart was broken and the relationship was over.

A few days after the sad Santa event, the boy had to make a trip to the outdoor toilet. On his way back to the classroom, Etoin, one of his older classmates who Rock thought of as being "dirty to the point of being rusty," accosted him. She tried to lure him into the crawl space under the schoolhouse and proposed to engage in a form of illicit sexual activity the boy had heard some of the older boys speak about. His answer of "No" was definitely made much easier by his knowledge that Etoin had recently had both scabies and head lice.

That proposition to the boy, however minuscule the temptation, became the absolute clincher…Rock was finished with girls.

DECISIONS ROCK THE BOAT

When a farm-boy turned eight in those days so heavily affected by the depression, many of them graduated from having a few simple assigned chores to performing as a full-time farmhand. Rock thought it was something special when his father first allowed him to plow a mule on their family farm (a farm that would eventually become part of the sprawling Atlanta International Airport). They did not assign him the intricate jobs that required great skill, but more menial tasks like preparing the land with a turning-plow or "busting the middles" with a scooter and scrape. This brought a new, unhappy relationship with a female into his life. She came in the form of a black Spanish mule known by the very simple name of Blackie.

In the boy's opinion, she was absolutely the most stubborn living thing in the whole world. Pairing Blackie's stubbornness with Rock's instant redheaded temper produced daily—no, hourly, and sometimes much more frequent—confrontations. From the beginning of their relationship, trying to work those two together seemed like trying to mix fire and gasoline.

It took a completely new vocabulary for the boy to speak to a mule as stubborn as Blackie, and Rock soon learned every word contained in that vile vocabulary. Every day as he plowed, he walked the very thin line between the apparent necessity to use foul language and the fear that his mother or father might hear him, or someone might report him. Of the two parents, he had much more fear of his mother. She was the one who carried the rod of instant chastisement and, having never regularly plowed a mule, she would never understand the necessity of the boy's using that particular language in the event someone told her about it.

Spring turned to summer and the relationship of boy to mule went from bad to worse. Rock felt really ashamed for using the vile language, but he seemed powerless to control his tongue when he was angry at that mule. Of course, he blamed it all on the mule. "If she would just not be so doggone stubborn, I wouldn't have to talk to her like that," he whined in his imperfect logic.

With the advent of late summer and the laying by of crops, the Cooper Street Baptist Church scheduled an old-fashioned Baptist revival meeting, as it usually did at this season each year. When the revival started, the weather, the church building and the evangelistic preaching were all equally hot. As he sat in his front-row seat, the boy quickly noticed with amusement that the light from the schoolhouse-globe lamp hanging above the preacher's head reflected a reddish glare on the shiny bald scalp of Rev. Q. L. Fry, the fiery evangelist. All windows in the church were wide open to let in any cool breeze that might blow by, and to let the preaching out so those who passed by could hear. The preacher had warmed up to the point of beginning to wipe sweat from his brow and gasp for his breath, when another wave of preaching fervor struck him. About this time, a huge tumblebug flew in through an open window.

The amusement of the light reflecting from the preacher's shiny dome now became secondary as the huge insect zoomed toward the bright light and began to fly in circles around it. Around and around the light and near the preacher's bald head it went for 100 or more concentric revolutions. The boy almost felt seasick from following the bug's orbital path from the vantage point of his front-row seat.

According to the laws of physics, it is impossible for an object of this shape, proportion and weight to fly, but that bug had never studied physics. However, there is a definite limit to the length of time such a large insect can maintain flight, and this bug apparently had neared his flight limit.

Seeking a place to land, the large critter chose the closest location, Rev. Fry's bald dome. Rock watched in shocked boyish amusement as the bug's landing gear found no source of traction for landing on that preacher's slick and shiny pate. It seemed to skid for a short distance, then it catapulted end-over-end through the air until it crashed in the center aisle in front of the pulpit and lay there helplessly on its back with its legs hopelessly clawing for any source of traction.

A titter went through the congregation and every eye was fixed directly on Rev. Fry as he stood there breathless and trying to keep his composure for what seemed to the boy an eternity. Unable to control himself, he finally erupted in a great guffaw of even louder volume than his most fervent Baptist, evangelistic, four-point sermon could ever reach.

There was neither an altar call nor the usual singing of 14 verses of *Just as I Am* or *I Surrender All* at the end of that service. No sinners came to give their hand to Preacher Gillem and their heart to Jesus, either. Through his tears of uncontrollable laughter, Rev. Fry simply pronounced the benediction.

The nightly meetings resumed the following night and moved into full swing. Rock's father spoke to the boy that day about his need to accept Jesus Christ as his Savior. "Son," said Newton, "you are eight years old and have heard about Jesus all your life. You know the difference between right and wrong and you probably know of some things in your own life that are not right. Those things are called 'sins' and, the Bible says, 'The wages of sin is death.' Don't you think it's about time for you to ask Jesus to come into your heart and forgive you of your sins, and for you to join the Church?"

"Yessir, Daddy," came the boy's immediate reply.

Rock already felt badly about the way he talked to Blackie every day, and he had even talked to God about it quite a number of times in his prayers. Now, he was absolutely convinced those curse words were the things that would condemn him and send him straight to Hell if he did not repent and change his way of talking.

The next night at the protracted meeting (a term some people used for revivals in those days) he could hardly wait to go down front, shake Preacher Gillem's hand, and tell him how much he wanted to be saved. He was glad Preacher Gillem did not make him enumerate the sins he was confessing in front of all those people, especially his Mother and Daddy. Perhaps, since he had been able to keep the exact nature of his sinful acts a secret, his Mother and Daddy would not find out what kind of words he had been saying. In that case, he might well be spared a fate at least more immediate than, if not worse than, hell's fire.

After asking Jesus to come into his heart, Rock felt so much better. It was as if someone had lifted a heavy weight both from his shoulders and from his mind. As he placed the harness on Blackie's strong shoulders the following morning to begin another day of plowing, the boy felt even cleaner than he did on those Saturday nights when he was allowed to be the first in line to use the family bath water.

"Blackie," he said, in a much gentler voice than his normal brusque tone, "I'm sorry for the way I've talked to you so many times in the past. I want you to know I'm a Christian now and I ain't gonna talk to you that way anymore."

Having bared his heart to his mule and made a solemn promise not to "cuss" her any more, Rock proceeded with his plowing partner to a nearby patch of new-ground that his Daddy had ordered him to prepare for planting turnip seed. The turnip greens would provide the family with food for the fall and the turnips, themselves, would be winter food.

He had just put the plow-point into the ground and Blackie had pulled it only a few short feet when the plow struck a root and stopped abruptly, jolting the boy with great force. He felt a great sense of pride in himself for holding his tongue as he stumbled and nearly fell to the ground with the sudden impact. He viewed this as a sign that he stood on the brink of final victory over this sinful habit called "cussin'."

After he had freed the plow from the root, Rock told Blackie, "Giddup." The mule did not move. "I said giddup," Rock bellowed as he struck her lightly on the flank with a plow line. This time, the mule and plow moved forward and Rock basked in the glow of the gleaming halo he envisioned himself to be wearing as an award for not using one of those accursed words in that situation. After a few more feet of progress, there was another jolting stop and, this time, the plow handle struck Rock quite hard in the lower abdomen.

"D...," muttered the redhead as he writhed in pain. Then, the much more intense emotional pain consumed him as he realized he had badly tarnished his halo, if it had not fallen off completely. "Mr. Perfectly Clean" from the night before was not so clean any more.

Before he finished plowing that small parcel of new-ground, Rock had many encounters with roots and with that stubborn mule named Blackie. His tongue had slipped so many times; he had used every word in his "cussin'" vocabulary. He felt lower than a snake's belly…even lower than whale manure, which had to be on the bottom of the ocean. His "cleaner than clean" feeling had completely vanished.

Now, Rock was beginning to learn the hard fact that a boy's nature rarely changes just because he makes up his mind to be different, even as the result of some type of Christian conviction. In time, his understanding would become more complete that it takes the work of a much higher power than he could ever be, working from the inside to change any person.

For the next couple of years, Rock made little or no progress in his battle against cussin', his greatest vice. As he was forced to continue to plow Blackie, his inability to control that sin often caused him to doubt whether Jesus really lived in his heart, what with his temper tantrums and his frequent choice of wrong words aimed at that darned old mule. The redhead became absolutely convinced that Satan had embodied himself in that stubborn Spanish hybrid and she had no other job except to tempt him. Nor could Satan gain any greater pleasure than by seeing the boy fall flat on his face in his effort to live a perfect life. How Rock wished his Daddy would sell that mule.

One of the good things about living in Mountain View was that the boy had to plow only three days a week. On Tuesday, Thursday and Saturday, his Mother would have the family car loaded with whatever vegetables and fruits were available for sale. She would then take little Rosa and Rock with her on a produce route in Hapeville. Rock felt as if he had become quite a polished salesman each time he recited verbatim the great sales pitch his mother had diligently taught him, "Ma'am, would you like to buy some nice pole beans? They're as pretty as a June bride and as tender as a mother's love."

This tri-weekly endeavor provided some much needed income for the family. It also gave the lad some welcome respite from his constant nemesis, Blackie.

Another source of relief the redhead found in Mountain View was an area on the farm where a small creek was piped through a culvert underneath the railroad track. Over the years, the water's constant fall from the culvert had washed out a small area where the water was deep enough for swimming. After studying the contour of the land, the older boys conceived the idea that a very small dam in the creek below this deep hole would produce a much larger and deeper impoundment. They built the dam and very creatively christened their creation as "the wash-hole."

Rock could not give much help to the other boys as they constructed their dam but, even though he could not swim, he was among the first to play in the cool water after it was impounded. His older brother, James, tried patiently for quite a while in an attempt to teach the clumsy, frightened redhead the art of swimming.

Finally, in desperation, James threw the boy into the deepest part of the impounded water and told him to get out by himself or drown. Angry, frightened, coughing, crying and sputtering, the boy dog paddled to safety, but he could swim after a sort. Unfortunately, he never advanced much beyond the dogpaddle in the art of swimming.

The wash-hole became a popular place for all the boys in the community. It was great fun to stand on top of the culvert that carried the stream under the railroad, and dive head first or belly-bust into the water. Rock thought it was even more fun to crawl through to the upper end of the culvert where he would turn around and lay flat on his belly. The flowing water would then carry him through the slippery, sloping, algae-coated culvert and dump him head first into the water. Only a few of the boys owned bathing suits in those depression days and it became the accepted norm to skinny-dip at the wash-hole.

The boys throughout the community soon found out about the swimming hole and made so much ado about their good times that the girls became jealous and demanded they be given equal time. Tuesday and Thursday afternoons were assigned to girls, but the family soon abandoned those plans. A majority of girls also had no bathing suits, and there were too many hiding places for gawking boys. The family and the community frowned sternly on this public pubic exposure, so this venture soon ended.

During a very bad dry spell in 1935, the family raised the dam even higher, causing the water to rise to a point where they could divert it from its normal banks into trenches they had dug by hand. These trenches carried the water into the fields where they diverted it into individual rows for irrigation of the drought-stricken corn. What had begun as simply a lark for the boys in the family and had become a much appreciated source of recreation for the boys in the community, now became a great asset for the family as a whole, because the makeshift irrigation saved that vital corn crop.

About three times a week, a passenger train came chugging down the track (the boys called it a "try weakly") and quite a scene would unfold when a group of guys were skinny dipping. Some of the boys would hide in the bushes, some ran for the culvert and others headed for the deep water. After a couple of swimming seasons, some of the older boys from the neighborhood did not make any attempt to hide their naked bodies from the passing trains. In fact, a few of them stood in the open and waved at the passengers.

This angered the railroad and, since the deepest part of the impoundment was on their right-of-way, they responded by dumping a large load of broken glass into the water near their culvert. Rock greatly mourned the loss of his place to swim but, at least, the family could still use the water for their crude irrigation system if it became necessary.

Rock continued to do well in the classroom at Mountain View School. He remained a favorite of his teacher, Miss Hood, an old maid who had no siblings and who still resided with her parents. The Hood trio regularly attended the same church that Rock's family attended. Rock's father and Miss Hood's father both served as deacons in the church. Newton called every adult male member "Brother"…so did the boy. As he was learning the words to the patriotic song, *America the Beautiful*, it created a dilemma for the redhead. With great gusto but with little understanding, he would voice the words "and crown thy good with 'brotherhood.'" At the same time, the naïve boy wondered how his school teacher's father fit into the words of the patriotic song they sang so frequently.

April Fool's day was a special day when most boys, and a few girls, slipped out of the classroom when the teacher turned her back. Then, they played hooky for the remainder of the school day. Rock had always resisted any temptation to leave, but he had secretly felt like a sissy for not joining his classmates in the custom. Most of the other boys also considered him a sissy, and frequently told him so.

"They haven't got the mother I've got," the redhead would often repeat under his breath. "She would kill me if she ever caught me doing anything like that."

But the boy was growing up—already in the fifth grade. This appeared to be the perfect time for him to do it, if he was ever going to gain the respect of his peers. Besides, Miss Hood had been gone from the room for several minutes, and it was almost noon. He would certainly not miss anything of importance in his school work if he left now. So, out the window slid the redhead and he raced across the schoolyard. When he reached the briar patch surrounding the school, he stopped to think. *I haven't planned any place to go and I surely don't want to smoke any of that ol' rabbit tobacco the other boys are smoking*, so he ran back across the schoolyard and bolted through the open door.

He got back to his seat just in the nick of time as the door opened and in came a smiling Miss Hood. She brought one of those new type treats called Hunky Bars for each student who "had not abandoned their school studies for foolhardy and useless adventure."

A broad smile showed through Rock's chocolate-covered face as he considered, *I have had the best of both worlds. I had the adventure of leaving school and not being caught. The boys will respect me for that. Now I get Miss Hood's praise and a Hunky Bar for not leaving. How lucky can any one boy be?*

However, Rock had taken pride in an action his mother would have considered "un-Christian," and his conscience began to hurt him. Even though he had been able to hide the April Fool's Day incident from his mother, he wrestled hard with his conscience in an attempt to justify what had happened.

The boy reasoned aloud as if someone else were present, "Why is what I did in leaving school any worse than the story she told me about Mr. Jim Bob Gladstone? But Mother says what he did was 'God's will and a real blessing to the whole community.'

"She told me that Mr. Jim Bob had told this story about his ol' cow going dry. He was out of work and his kids didn't have anything to eat, so they killed the cow and sold some of the meat. They ate the rest, but it didn't last very long, and he still couldn't find any work. He was afraid his whole family would starve and he didn't have but 15 cents to his name. That night he had this really weird dream that seemed so real to him he didn't believe he was dreaming. He kept seeing the numbers five, four, and seven everywhere he turned.

"It woke him up from a sound sleep and he couldn't sleep the rest of the night. Next morning he climbed out of bed real early and could not wait to tell his wife about his 5-4-7 dream, and ask what she thought those numbers might mean.

"Well, his wife said she thought it was a message from God and He was trying to answer their prayers for help in these troubling times. She said, 'I think you ought to take a nickel of our money and play it on the 'bug' (an illegal lottery based on the last three numbers of three daily stock or government reports) and use the numbers 5-4 and 7. I know us Christians ain't supposed to gamble, but when the Lord gives you the numbers, what else can you do?'

"Sure enough, Mr. Jim Bob walked five miles to Hapeville and put a nickel on 5-4 and 7. Then, he walked the five miles back home and waited, but those numbers didn't fall. Next day, he walked back to Hapeville and played the same numbers again leaving him only one nickel in his pocket. They failed to fall again. Now, he had walked 20 miles and spent down to his last nickel, so he asked his wife again, 'What should I do?'

"She said, 'Well, Jim Bob, we trusted the Lord down to our last nickel, now I think we should trust Him with our last nickel.'

"So that's just what he did. He marched those five miles to 'the bug' agent's house and laid down his last nickel. He says he prayed all the way home and couldn't hardly wait for the paper to come out. Lo and behold, the numbers were 5-4 and 7 and he won enough money to buy a cow that had just freshened and get enough feed to take care of her for a year.

"When Mr. Jim Bob talks about it, he says, 'It was in the month of June an' I won her on 'the bug,' so I named her 'June Bug.'

"Shoot, if you ask me, what that ol' man did was just plain ol' gambling. He comes to church almost every Sunday and he stands up and prays so pious like. How did he know about 'the bug' and where he could go to play the thing in the first place?' Preacher

Gillem says it ain't nothing but an instrument of ol' Satan himself, and no Christian ought to ever be caught playing it.

"Mother says she thinks it came as 'God's revelation to Mr. Gladstone for the good of his family, and it kept the community from having to support another family in these tough times.' She says God used 'the bug' to show ol' Satan he ain't in complete control of anything, and He took Satan's money to serve God's purpose, and she says it's a downright miracle.

"Well, if the Lord told him to gamble, then I think the Lord kept me from getting caught when I left school on April's fool day…but I don't ever want to go through anything like that again."

Rev. Allison, the principal of Mountain View School, also served as teacher of the seventh grade. An ordained Baptist minister, he had been quite an athlete in college, and he loved to join in baseball games with his seventh grade boys. The boy had never seen anyone except his brother, James, who could hit a baseball as far as Rev. Allison. He thought it might be a little out of character that Rev. Allison, both a preacher and an athlete, should smoke cigars…but then, his own father also smoked King Edward cigars and taught Sunday School.

One day in a game on the school grounds Rev. Allison hit a long drive, certain to be a home run. He rounded first and then second base at top speed. His tightly buttoned vest kept his tie in place, but his sparse hair, kept long to cover his nearly bald head, blew straight back in the wind. About midway between second and third base, the school principal suddenly stopped and fell to his knees in the red clay. He began clutching and beating the area of his right groin. Many of the students dashed toward their principal, fearing he might be severely injured.

Smiles of relief showed in their faces when the students learned that the heads of stick matches he carried in his pocket to light his cigars had rubbed together and ignited. The biggest tragedy was that the matches had set fire to a ten-dollar bill he had in his pocket.

In addition, they had burned a hole in his pocket and produced a painful burn on Rev. Allison's right thigh. To add to his indignity, the outfielders chased down the ball and hurried it back into the infield. In spite of his monumental clout, the principal was tagged out.

The boy's low self-esteem that continued because of his poor athletic prowess and his seemingly uncontrollable cussin' was driven even lower by his equally uncontrollable gluttony. At church suppers and family reunions, he would eat until he regurgitated, then return to the table. This sin was not overlooked by many older people in the community, and he was often referred to as "that hog."

His feelings of guilt were not in any way assuaged by the event in the daily chapel service one morning as Rev. Allison presided. The fact that these meetings were held each day caused every school principal to have a problem with providing content that was always upbuilding. This was the case on this particular morning.

Rev. Allison stood at the podium and said, "I came around the corner of the school building yesterday and heard someone crying. I followed the sounds and found Rock Notleks between the shrubbery and the school building crying his eyes out. I asked him, 'Rock, what in the world is wrong?'

"Rock looked up at me with tears dripping off his chin and said, 'Reverend Allison, somebody has stolen every dab of my lunch except for thirteen baked sweet potatoes.'"

March winds were intense that year and succeeded in blowing the roof completely off the family's two-holer outhouse. Several months elapsed before they could restore the roof and anyone who used the facility for necessary accommodations sat in peril of sun, snow, sleet and rain. While the structure remained without a top, Rock ran down its path one day feeling a strong urge to empty his bladder. He found the door latched and his older brother, James, in occupancy. Rock knocked on the door. "Open up, Jimmy," he called, "Open up. I'm about to bust."

"You can wait a minute," James echoed.

The boy's legs were crossed, but not because he was lying. "I can't hold it much longer," he said. "I told you, I'm about to bust."

"Well, you'll just have to wait. I can't get up now," the unwanted reply resounded. "If you've just got to pee, go behind the outhouse. Nobody will see you there."

"You'll be sorry," Rock moaned as he stepped into the tall weeds behind the outhouse, being quite careful to look for any evidence of snakes. Seeing none of the slithering varmints, he took careful aim at the open outhouse roof.

Only a few drops of slightly yellow liquid had rained through its large roof aperture when the outhouse door flew open. Still securing his overalls, James bolted out in hot pursuit of the boy, who had suddenly forgotten the intensity of pain from his distended bladder while fleeing the more intense pain of James' wrath.

The race did not last long before the groveling redhead cringed on the ground under his brother's raised fist, crying in tearful anticipation of the beating he richly deserved from the offended sibling. "You little so-and-so, I ought to kill you…But then," said James as he laughed and released his grip, "I should have unlatched the door."

This incident only served to raise the level of admiration the grateful boy already felt for his older brother. Now, Rock must add "the kindest person in the world" to the list of accolades he had for his idol and benefactor.

He already considered Jimmy to be the strongest, the fastest and the most athletic young man in the whole world—and why shouldn't he? This hero had already proved those things beyond any reasonable person's doubt. He was Golden Gloves Boxing champion of Clayton County, the star player on Jonesboro High's football team and a starter on the basketball team, and he did whip that bozo, Big Bruno, at the Clayton County fair. How Rock loved to relate those stories of his brother's athletic prowess.

Given any opportunity, the boy would brag, "Man, is he strong. He can grab me by the coat lapel and lift me off the ground with just one arm—and he does it without even bending his elbow.

"Mother told him she didn't want him to be in any kind of fighting sport, but he went out for Golden Gloves boxing in Clayton County anyhow. He won the county championship without ever having enough of a mark on him for Mother to find out he was boxing. When the Golden Gloves committee told him he should go to the state tournament, he said, 'No sir. Those reports might get into the Atlanta newspaper, and then Mother might find out what I have been doing.'

"He's not afraid of any guy in the county…but Mother…now that's a different story.

"In his senior year of high school at Jonesboro, Jimmy went out for the first football team they ever had. The players just lined off a place on the school playground with lime and cut down some saplings to make their goal posts, and they were ready to play. They didn't have any uniforms and certainly no lights. The team had to play their games in the afternoon against teams from schools that were just about as poor as Jonesboro. They didn't charge admission, but few people ever watched them play. Everybody had to work because of the depression. Mr. Jernigan was the coach and he had Jimmy playing tailback.

"One day when they were playing Forest Park, a black limousine pulled up and two men got out of the car to watch the game. They pulled out the first two folding chairs any of us country folks had ever seen and sat while they watched the teams play. When the game was over, one of the men came up to Jimmy and said, 'I'm Wallace Butts. I coach football at the University of Georgia and would like to offer you a scholarship to come and play for me at the University of Georgia.'

"Jimmy didn't wait a second before he answered, 'No thank you, sir. I ain't going to college. I'm going to be a farmer.'

"It's the dumbest thing my brother ever did. Can't you just see him right now playing football with Frankie Sinkwich and Charlie Trippi? Why, I hear they even have a chance to go to the Rose Bowl this year and that's way out west, off yonder in California. He passed up the chance to go to California just to stay home and plow a stupid old mule."

ROCK, Further Proof of God's Sense of Humor

Rock became extremely excited about the fair that visited each year in Clayton County because they gave free admission to all school children. That year his mother even gave him 50 cents to spend. She said he had earned it selling so many pole beans.

At the fair, the clumsy boy soon learned of his hidden talent to operate the machine where you put in a nickel and tried to pickup coins with an apparatus like a grappling claw. This talent soon tripled his funds for the fair but, more importantly, it became his first insight into the fact he had some innate ability to perform at least one intricate physical task.

James quickly abandoned his younger brother at the fair and ran off with his peers in their own pursuits. Because of this, Rock was not an eyewitness as the following drama unfolded, but he loved to tell the story as if he had seen every dramatic scene.

"'Step right up, Ladies and Gentlemen,' the sideshow announcer barked into his megaphone. 'Yes, step right up and see Big Bruno from Germany, the future heavyweight champion of the world.' As the Clayton County Golden Gloves champion, Jimmy naturally had an interest in this boxing phenom and urged his friends to stop with him outside Big Bruno's tent.

"'Big Bruno will take on any and all challengers,' the barker continued his harangue, 'and you can see all the action inside for just ten cents. In fact, if you are willing to take on Big Bruno and are able to stay in the ring with him for only three rounds, you will receive not five, ten or twenty dollars, but the amazing sum of twenty-five dollars. Just imagine—that is almost three dollars a minute. Where else can you make big money like that?

"'Big Bruno gives his solemn promise not to maul anyone' the barker's spiel went on. 'Why you can throw in the towel anytime you have had enough. Just think of all you could do with twenty-five dollars.'

When no one climbed into the ring after the announcer offered such big money, Big Bruno grabbed the megaphone.

'You're all cowards,' he bellowed; but still, nobody from the crowd would volunteer.

"Big Bruno began to point to different faces in the crowd and just kept on hollering in that megaphone. 'You're a coward,' he sneered as he pointed to Howard. 'You're a coward,' he yelled as he pointed to Leonard. 'You're a coward,' he hollered as if he was disgusted and he pointed to Jimmy.

"One thing no one ever dared to do was to call my brother a coward. Jimmy jerked off his jacket in a hurry as he climbed into the ring with that big ol' professional boxer. Man, it looked like Mutt and Jeff. Jimmy stood five feet and nine inches and weighed not quite 160 pounds against Big Bruno, who measured about six feet two and weighed over 230 pounds.

"Everybody started hollering for Jimmy and calling Big Bruno a bully for picking on such a small boy, but Jimmy kept circling to his left and sort of jabbing his left hand. just staying out of the big guy's way. Big Bruno kept yelling at Jimmy, 'Why don't you stand still and fight. Stop runnin' like a coward, but Jimmy just kept circling and jabbing with his left.

"Then, all of a sudden it happened. Jimmy lashed out with his right hand and caught the big ol' guy right on the point of his chin. His knees buckled and Big Bruno fell to the floor. I told you it looked like Mutt and Jeff, but it seemed more like David and Goliath.

"Call it a lucky punch, an act of fate or whatever you want to call it; Jimmy knocked that ol' Big Bruno out in the very first round. When he tried to collect his reward of twenty-five dollars, the manager told him, 'But you didn't stay for the three rounds you were supposed to stay to get the money.'"

After this event, many others in the community joined Rock in his adulation of his idol and older brother, James. Wherever he went, people referred to James as 'the giant killer,' a term he came to despise.

GROWING UP IS HARD AS A ROCK

Many people, especially the young girls in the county who swooned over Jimmy, considered it a tragedy when economic reasons forced the family to move again; this time to Ben Hill. The Mountain View farm had become less productive and the family needed another place where they could clear new-ground for farming. Rock demonstrated much more elation about the move to Ben Hill than any other member of his family showed. Not only was he putting behind him forever the degrading memories of both June Dane and Etoin, but there existed a far greater reason for his show of happiness.

"Gosh, Jimmy," exclaimed the emotional redhead in his most excited tone of voice that he usually reserved for Christmas, "Have you heard the fantastic news? Daddy is going to trade Blackie for a heavier mare. I won't ever have to plow that tormenting black hussy again. Maybe I'll be able to stop my cussin' now. I'm certain no other mule in the world could ever be as stubborn as she is. I really do believe the old Devil, himself, is embodied in that mule."

Never mind the fact he must leave his small circle of good male friends, especially Bud Johnson. Blackie would be absent from his daily routine. Because of that one fact, life had never seemed so sweet.

The boy felt quite grown up as he enrolled in Sandtown Grammar School: already 11 years old, in the seventh grade, the oldest of the three family members to transfer there. He smiled broadly as he presented his sixth-grade report cards to the principal as evidence of his academic achievements. At the same time, he secretly rejoiced that he did not need reports concerning his emotional maturity, his self-esteem or his athletic prowess.

To the boy, Mrs. Wingo, the school principal, looked to be ancient as he handed her those report cards. He would have to watch her quite closely to see how anyone so decrepit could possibly function even as a teacher, much less in her dual capacity as a principal.

As he boarded the bus for home that first afternoon, he asked his younger sisters, "Did you ever see as many wrinkles and gray hairs on any one person as Mrs. Wingo has? I don't remember us reading anywhere in the Bible or any of those Bible-story books we've got at home about her being on Noah's Ark, but she sure must 'a been there.

"I'll tell you one thing for certain, that woman scares me to death. She always carries that big ol' ruler in her hand, and she knows just how and where to use it too, I'll bet. Thank goodness, she didn't hafta' use it on me, and she ain't goin' to either. I'd hate to have her tear me up and then Mother do it again when I got home. If she's gotta be my teacher, I sure am glad I don't have but one year to stay in this place."

Despite his brash, cocky and confident exterior when talking with his family, the redhead remained a wretched wreck internally. He considered himself the biggest glutton, the worst cry baby and, in any game or exercise that required some degree of grace or skill, the most awkward participant that ever existed in this world. Also, he felt as if he had become a bully because of his tendency to pick on boys in the sixth, or even sometimes the fifth grade. Not even once did he consider the fact these boys were actually his peers in age and physical maturity.

On the first day of school, the local kids made the redhead feel good by taking him as the third person chosen for the baseball game during recess. Being unfamiliar with his lack of coordination and noting only his relatively large frame, they took a chance on his athleticism.

How the boy's heart pounded in his first at bat. Even he fully believed he would knock a home run and score those two men on base in front of him—but that was not to be the case. In his excitement over the game, he struck out as usual. Nor would he field a high percentage of the balls hit in his direction when his team played in the field.

In just a few short days, every student in the Sandtown School became aware of Rock's ineptness in any type of sports. Then the situation went back to the old "You take him," "No, you take him" routine each time a team was chosen. The boy felt miserable once again, although he still unrealistically held to a hope that "this is sure to be my time to show them how good I am" every time he got up to bat or took the field.

In the classroom, he continued to hold his own quite well, and soon became one of Mrs. Wingo's favorites, especially after she learned that Christine Wilson, another member of the class, could read the hieroglyphic scribbling the boy passed off as writing. Mrs. Wingo's policy allowed the students to correct and grade one another's daily papers. She corrected only the big test papers, and it made her job much easier. Most students passed their papers each day to a different person to cut down on the possibility of cheating. Since no one but Christine could read the redhead's writing, the same girl now graded his papers every day, and that caused the boy a great deal of worry.

He reasoned as he worried: *If she ever learns how I really feel about girls, Christine might make a few extra errors on grading my papers just to get even with me. On the other hand, if I act as if I like her, she might want to go steady or something.* It was quite a difficult position for a boy to find himself in when his real desire in life was to hate girls. Rock decided that his best course of action would be to just be cautious, act friendly and see what happened. He surely did not want or need any girlfriend at this stage of his life.

A short while later, some friends at church told him that Christine liked a boy who was a sophomore in high school and they were supposed to be going steady. This information caused the worried lad to breathe a great sigh of relief and his mood brightened considerably. For the remainder of the seventh grade, he felt reasonably comfortable with the grading arrangement, although he kept up his guard against encouraging any relationship with Christine beyond that of being normal classmates.

"You know, you just can't really tell how these girls will take anything you say or do," he confided to his cousin, Jesse, whose family had quickly followed Rosa and Newton to the Ben Hill area to continue what Rock considered their parasitic relationship.

New Hope Baptist Church was less than a mile from the family's home—within easy walking distance. This created a new situation for the boy, whose family had always had to travel much further for their religious activities. Heretofore, Sunday had meant being crowded into the family car with all the seemingly necessary singing, teasing, tattling, bickering and sitting on one another's laps while traveling more than 30 minutes to church. This had not been conducive to an attitude of real worship on arrival at the church. Now the boy could avoid those family confrontations by striking out on foot, especially if he feared being late or if the family had left him behind because of his own dawdling tardiness.

The fervent evangelical preaching of Pastor Howard Johnson and the simple, quiet teaching of her Sunday school class by the pastor's wife, Bessie, along with the location of the church being closer to their home, soon stirred the entire family into more active participation in church activities than ever before. Newton and Rosa were both soon teaching Sunday school classes. Little Rosa became the church pianist and played for several singing groups within the church and within the family.

James often led the congregational singing and he joined with Rosa and the Galloway boys to form a quartet that performed at many events in the community. Rock thought they were better than most of the groups he heard on The Grand Old Opry when he could get that show on the crystal set radio.

Helen and Mary Lou joined with Rock and "Pud" Cole, Jr., to form a kid's quartet that sang at many church or community events with little Rosa as pianist. The baby, Ethel, too young and squirmy to be in any organized singing group, felt free to join any one of them, much to the boy's dismay and embarrassment. He had to admit, she didn't do too badly for a snotty-nosed brat. She knew all the words, and always sang the part that was in the lead at the time. Everybody but the redhead thought it was cute.

With each member of the family involved in church activities, religious fervor in the family rose to an all-time high. Virtually all of the free time away from farm labor had already been ticketed for these activities, prompting Rosa to quote a poem that Rock always believed she had penned with her own hand:

> Mary had a little lamb.
> It would have been a sheep.
> But, then, it joined a Baptist Church
> and died for lack of sleep.

During this period of intense church activity, a young female missionary gave a report to the church about her mission activities. James seemed to be extremely impressed by her presentation and by the young lady, also. A few days later, he came from his work in the field one evening and made an announcement that startled the family. "I believe God is calling me to go to Africa as a missionary," he said.

Rocks immediate reaction became, "Wow, I wish it could have been me."

In his boyish mind and heart, Rock already missed his older brother, but he could not help thinking, *Africa? Man, maybe Jimmy knew what he was doing when he turned down the chance to play football at Georgia and go out to California. California ain't nothing compared to Africa.*

At the same time, he wondered, *Am I jealous of the attention Jimmy is getting?* He had never before recognized any jealousy toward Jimmy in himself…only a feeling of great admiration.

The redhead had no concept of what being a missionary meant, but he pondered his older brother's decision for several weeks and could never completely dismiss those thoughts from his mind. He had always wanted to do exactly the same things Jimmy did, but he always felt his efforts in no way equaled those of his hero and gifted brother. *Are these thoughts coming into my mind because I want to copy Jimmy*, he mused, or, *could it be possible that God is really calling me to be a missionary, too?*

Rock waited long enough for the newness of Jimmy's announced calling to wear off, hoping no one would suspect his possible copycat motives. Then, he made the announcement, "I believe God is calling me to be a medical missionary to Bolivia."

The boy had no idea where to look on a map to find Bolivia—only that it existed somewhere in the world, and his ignorance was not only geographical; he had no idea of how one would begin a journey to become a doctor, or how long that process might take. He only knew his "calling" had to be different enough from that of Jimmy for folks not to see through any possible façade, so he chose a different country-and a more specific field. In this illogical manner, he began his journey toward a medical career.

From that point on, and for a period of several years thereafter, any time Rock attended a religious gathering that gave a call for full-time-Christian-service volunteers, he would be the first to respond. Oh, how badly the redhead hoped God would join him in his self-appointed journey into missionary service. However, he never had any doubts about the genuineness of his call into medicine, but he did not know what a difficult path that entailed.

Like all other schools of that time, Sandtown School featured a daily chapel service. Mrs. Wingo seemed poorly prepared for this function as a school principal. At times, she resorted to an amateur hour format where students could demonstrate their talents to other students. Rock looked forward to these events with mixed emotions. It meant he had to suffer again as the Pulaski sisters did their very nasal a cappella version of Maple-on-a-Hill. On the other hand, he could do his rousing rendition of one of the many poems he had memorized, for example, *I Hate it When Folks Call Me Son*. He had even performed that one on WSB radio.

The boy could hardly believe his eyes when, near the end of one of these amateur sessions, he saw his cousin, Jesse, walking toward the stage. Jesse had never volunteered for anything in his lifetime. He had certainly never shown any talent that impressed the redhead. Why would he—of all people—be headed for the stage? Rock wondered.

Jesse mounted the stairs, took a left turn and walked to the center of the stage. With his eyes cast directly on the floor, Jesse rocked back and forth from the heels to the toes of his brogan shoes and began his recitation:

> "I had an old mule.
> I fed him on corn.
> He hiked his tail
> and blowed his horn."

In spite of her ancient years, Mrs. Wingo immediately sprang onto the stage like Mighty Mouse. She grabbed Jessie by the nape of his neck and filled his ear so loudly the whole student body could hear every word as she led him to the Principal's office. "Jesse Turnblow, you have disgraced the Sandtown School."

After his brief suspension, Jesse told Rock in strict confidence that some of the other boys had put him up to this bit of mischief and had even given him a quarter for his efforts. A quarter did not represent a small sum in those days. The redhead holds no memory of Mrs. Wingo's having allowed any other amateur hours during the remainder of that school year.

The family farming operation in Ben Hill was somewhat different from the one they had used in Mountain View. Instead of disposing of the crops by selling them retail on a produce route, it now became a wholesale operation with sales by the bushel or even by the truckload. The women in the household dutifully canned or cooked for immediate consumption any farm products that remained after the sale.

Only Jimmy and Rock remained as a family work force because all of the older boys had married and moved away from home. Now the family brought a hired man into the picture, and he added much flavor to life on the farm with his colorful stories, and the vocabulary he used to tell them.

Pitt Griggs (Rock called him "Uncle Pitt") was a black man, probably in his sixties but he looked much older. He had no known family. Uncle Pitt had been living in a small room in one of the outbuildings on the rented farm for a few years before Rock's family took over. Newton and Rosa contracted with him to continue to live in his room. He would work on the farm for his board and keep plus a small weekly stipend. He took his meals at the family home and sometimes ate with the family on the rare occasions that he arrived on time.

Uncle Pitt apparently had a very reliable and unending source of supply of so-called white lightning even in those days of prohibition, and it was a rare occasion when Pitt Griggs drew a sober breath. Uncle Pitt's stories about his boyhood escapades intrigued the boy greatly, although he believed very few of them. This black man's fondness for alcohol seemed to loosen both his imagination and his tongue.

The family soon learned that Uncle Pitt's fear of snakes loomed as strong as his love for alcohol. It haunted him day and night and, along with his age and alcoholism, it interfered greatly with his work on the farm. You did not ask Pitt Griggs to lift any object that might have a snake under it or to plow in a field where he had ever plowed up a snake in prior years, even a non poisonous one. These factors rendered him nearly useless as an employee. However, they did lead to some incidents that produced a great deal of laughter for the family and were often retold in family conversations.

On one particular day, most of the family and Uncle Pitt sat together on the front porch as they prepared sweet potato slips for planting in the waiting field that spring. James appeared quite excited as he came in for lunch. He had been by himself, digging drainage ditches in the bottomlands to have that area ready for planting later that spring.

"Boy, you should have seen that water moccasin. I'll bet he was at least six feet long and as big around as my arm," he said obviously shaken and wide eyed with wonder. "When I jumped across the ditch, I landed almost in the middle of him and he twisted around and bit right here in the top of my rubber boot. I managed to kill him, but if I had landed just two inches further back on his body, he would have gotten me right on the side of my knee."

Rock could hardly believe the fact that his idol had a fear of anything. "Gollee, Jimmy," he said with evident horror, "it's a good thing you had on those rubber boots. If you had been bitten by a snake as big as you say that one was, there ain't no way you'd have ever made it home by yourself, and we surely couldn't get an ambulance down into that swampy place, especially across that old rickety bridge."

Uncle Pitt broke up the conversation when he said, "Lawd, Mistah James, if a snake like that' un evuh come nearly that close to me, I wouldn't need no ambulance, but I sho' would need a laundry wagon."

Later that year, the boys and Uncle Pitt had gathered all of the crops and pulled up the peanut plants, which they stacked in an abandoned house on the farm with the peanuts still clinging to their roots. Rock still had a sad feeling about the vacant house because John Campbell had moved away and had taken the boys, Robin and Clyde, with him. John's two illegitimate grandsons had been the redhead's nearest and favorite playmates while they lived on the Ben Hill farm.

That October, when the workload became much lighter, Newton assigned Rock and Uncle Pitt to pick the peanuts off the dry vines. The task had just begun in earnest when the boy picked up an armful of the plants, and a small highland moccasin ran out from under them. The redhead picked up the only available weapon, a small stick that lay among the peanut plants, and chased after the snake.

"Hit 'im, Mr. Rock," Uncle Pitt yelled in encouragement as the snake ran to the opposite side of the room.

The boy chased the snake into one corner and Uncle Pitt retreated to the opposite corner as he yelled repeatedly, "Hit 'im, Mr. Rock."

Rock hated to admit that he harbored almost as much fear of the reptile as did Uncle Pitt. Clumsily, he chased the snake down the base of the wall again and noted Uncle Pitt now standing on the very top of the pile of peanut plants still on the opposite side of the room, screaming with all the volume of his coarse voice, "Hit 'im, Mr. Rock." The redhead could not remember a more comical sight.

The snake managed to slip through a small crack at the base of the wall and eluded the clumsy boy who used the excuse that he had only the flimsiest of sticks as a weapon. He failed to mention his shaking from both fear and laughter. In his bravado of snake chasing, he tried not to let his fear show.

The family promptly placed picking peanuts from pendant positions on peanut plants on the perpetual posting of projects for which Uncle Pitt perpetually parried petitions to perform. As the crops came and went that year, the family barely held its financial head above water.

The first quarter of his high school freshman year was nearly disastrous for the boy. In his opinion, the authors of The Ancient Mariner, Julius Caesar and some of those other literary works he had puzzled over that quarter might as well have written them in Greek. They certainly did not write in the "wood-box" English he had almost miraculously learned to read in the first grade. Nevertheless, he finally managed to recoup his losses and salvage a "C" in the course, his first mark below a "B" since he had gotten that "F" in reading in the first grade. After that, he finally learned the knack of how to study for his courses and was doing well at Russell High School.

Yes, things seemed on the upswing and the redhead looked forward to the future. His greatest problem for the moment lay with Sgt. Rathiewicz who stood in unquestioned charge of the ROTC (reserve officers training corps) program at Russell High. The sergeant insisted on each of his students wearing highly polished and shined shoes every day, regardless of any extenuating circumstances.

Rock definitely had an extenuating circumstance in that the WPA, the ultra-slow government Works Progress Administration, had selected the road where he lived, New Hope Church Road, for improvement. They hauled in tons of Georgia red clay to serve as a base for later top-soiling. This process took more than a year to complete and resulted in a broad expanse of red mud the boy had to cross every day to catch the bus for his one-hour ride to school. Each morning, he would leave his home wearing shoes so highly polished you could use them as a mirror. In dry weather, he might possibly arrive at school with his shoes prim and proper, but the slightest amount of moisture produced a sticky red mud that stuck to him like steel drawn to a magnet, and adhered like glue to everything—especially his shoes.

His tear-filled explanations to Sgt. Rathiewicz availed nothing—nor did notes from the boy's mother or even a visit to Sgt. Rathiewicz from that exalted lady. The Sergeant told Rock to wear another pair of shoes to board the bus, and then change to his shined pair. The thing the sergeant failed to comprehend was that the redhead did not own a second pair of shoes.

The boy finally reached a tenable solution by carrying his shoes and crossing the muddy road barefoot. Then he wiped his feet on the grass to remove the excess mud. As his feet got somewhat dry on the school bus, he would then put on his sock sand shoes. If Sgt. Rathiewicz had ever required him to remove his shoes and socks for inspection, he would have found that the redness of the boy's feet rivaled the redness of his hair; but the redhead survived that crisis and he learned.

As he marched down Atlanta's famous Peachtree Street in proper formation as part of the gala celebration of the world premier of *Gone with the Wind*, the redhead felt a great sense of pride, and was glad he had persisted in ROTC. In later years, he would come to have an even greater appreciation for the lessons he had learned in that venture.

Rock developed a very bad habit of procrastination in the early years of high school. He put most things off until the very last minute. Then he quickly and more sloppily than he had planned, threw something together and let it suffice. Even though this habit became deep rooted, he still maintained his good grades—God only knows why, if you looked at some of the gibberish in the materials he presented. However, on one particular occasion, he carried his procrastination act much too far.

A book report was due in Mr. Carroll's English class the following morning. As the boy went to bed the night before, he realized he had not even so much as checked out a book from the library on which to report. Moreover, he had not read a single page in any book recently to think of making a book report. This situation called for drastic action on the boy's part.

The next morning, he greeted his Mother's wake-up call with, "Mother, my stomach hurts."

"Rock, get up and eat your breakfast," Rosa echoed in reply. "You will feel better and then you can go to school."

"Mother, I don't want any breakfast this morning. I feel sick at my stomach," he said.

He already hated himself for his lying words of that moment, knowing well that both parts of his excuse were lies. However, he knew that reply would gain his Mother's immediate attention since he could never seem to get enough to eat.

"What is wrong with my baby boy?" Rosa said, using the phrase Rock hated most for her to call him. She sat on the side of his bed and pulled down the covers to feel his belly. The boy winced and falsely complained of pain with each soft touch of his abdomen by her loving hands.

"Okay, son," she said in final submission. "You just lie here while I get the other children ready for school. Then we'll find out exactly what is wrong."

Rock turned over in bed and feigned a fitful sleep. The sleep was feigned; the fitfulness came as a natural reaction to the fact that others were eating and he was not getting his share. This moment may have well been the boy's best theatrical performance of his lifetime.

The school bus came and the other children were off to school. When Rosa came back to see about Rock, she looked worried. He could hardly keep up his act, partly because he did not like what he was putting his Mother through and partly because he knew his breakfast had gotten cold by this time, if the others had not eaten it all.

Rosa sat on the side of Rock's bed and asked again, "What's the matter with my baby boy?"

As much as he hated that title, the boy knew that now would not be a proper time to complain. He also knew that it was much too early to claim a cure of all his symptoms. He knew his Mother would see through his little act and take him to face Mr. Carroll if his pain stopped at this moment.

"I don't know what's wrong, Mother," he lied in reply. "I just know that my belly hurts and I feel sick at my stomach."

Rosa laid her hands gently on the boy's abdomen again, only to have him wince and complain. Without hesitation, she informed her son, "Get out of bed and get dressed right now. We're going to Grady Hospital. We are not going to sit here and let your appendix burst like Jimmy's almost did"

On their arrival at the hospital, the staff quickly took Rock to the emergency room where a young doctor (Rock assumed him to be an intern) examined the boy and asked what seemed to be a million questions to the malingering redhead. His Mother answered most of these questions and never left the boy's side to give him an opportunity to level with his doctor. The doctor pressed hard enough on the boy's lower abdomen that it really did cause some pain at times, and the boy responded with grabbing the doctor's hand and nearly coming off the table.

At one point, the doctor even mentioned doing surgery to remove his appendix. The redhead would have been perfectly willing to let the situation go that far before he would admit to having staged the whole production to cover up his lack of a book report. It proved to be a ticklish situation and the boy had a lot to lose. *If only Mother would leave the room*, he thought, *I could level with this doctor and he might make it light on me*. However, his mother stayed constantly at his side.

Finally, the puzzled medic asked, "Did he ever pass a worm of any kind?"

Rock had no knowledge of any such incident, and shuddered at the thought. His Mother seemed to dig deep in her memory bank before she replied, "Yes, I believe we did find a worm in one of his bowel movements way back when he was about two or three years old, but he seemed okay and we didn't do anything about it."

"That's it," exclaimed the greatly relieved physician almost in a shout of jubilation. "He's got the worms."

Rock's sense of relief stood much greater and much more heartfelt than that of his doctor. He had just sidestepped the surgeon's blade and had done it with his secret remaining intact. Any medication the doctor might prescribe would be a minor cross to bear for such a major victory as he had just achieved. The boy stood ready to "take his medicine" in both the literal and the physical senses of the phrase.

By this time, the boy had adjusted his attitude to an outright eagerness to prepare his book report and regain his academic standing. He quaffed the terrible tasting medicine with a minimum of comment and resistance. He still did not have a book to read, and the library had already closed by this late hour, so he had to be creative.

Turning to his distant memory for a book to report on, he recalled a story that Miss Hood had read to the class four years earlier when he was in Mountain View. Try as hard as he might, the name of the author would not surface in his memory. In this desperate situation, he simply assigned the name of "Nathaniel Hawthorne" as the author of the work, and turned in his report the following morning. Now the boy had a few more days of worry to see if he had sneaked that fake paper by his sophomore English teacher. Apparently, Mr. Carroll was not familiar with the book and never noted the false name Rock had assigned as author of the work.

Rock felt he deserved the "A" he got on that paper as much as on any paper he had ever turned in. After all, it had caused him more problems in its preparation than any paper he had ever submitted in any subject (had almost cost him his appendix) but he vowed never to try that act again.

As the year 1939 began, the family had high hopes this year's crop would finally produce a reward for their hard labor on the farm. Although the interest rates remained exorbitant on the money they had borrowed, they had managed to exist and keep their creditors at bay in that era when the entire population was still depression poor. The bottomlands were finally in good shape and appeared to be quite fertile and all the uplands were clear and properly terraced. Both of the family's mules, Mollie and Maude, were high spirited, eager to work and well broken to the plow, and they were almost paid for. Even Rock had a new spirit about his work on the farm now that he approached 13 and the family had entrusted jobs requiring more responsibility to him.

Spring planting season arrived and the fields had been thoroughly prepared. James and Uncle Pitt had the rows laid out in proper order and the ground lay ready for fertilizer, which they had already loaded on a two-horse wagon. Rock had a grin from ear to ear as he held the reins in his hands to control the mules and issued a loud "Giddup" to Mollie and Maude. The boy tried to cover up the pride he felt in the fact that his Daddy had let him deliver the fertilizer to the bottomland area where the family planned to apply it the following day. He knew it was a very important job.

Perfect weather had made the job of soil preparation easier, and now it appeared that God had given an affirmative answer to the family's prayers for the final phase of planting. The boy whistled and/or sang happily, as the heavily loaded wagon rolled down the winding farm road and approached the bridge across the creek. He felt in total control of his crack team of mules. Every vestige of his past hatred of old Blackie had disappeared as Mollie and Maude pranced onto the bridge, followed quickly by the loaded wagon.

Suddenly, a very loud snapping sound shattered the serenity of his day. One of the main support logs for the bridge had broken completely in two under the weight of the mules. The boy watched in great horror as the right side of the bridge collapsed into the creek-bed. This caused Mollie to tumble into the water, laying on her right side. At the same instant, the force of the collapse virtually catapulted Maude across the bridge and she came to rest on top of Mollie.

"Oh, God, please help me," the redhead pleaded as he jumped from the wagon and onto the still standing portion of the bridge, not having any idea what he should do next. "Oh, God, please help me," he repeated again and again as he entered the water with the frightened mules. He was afraid that one of his own frightened animals might hurt him as they thrashed about in an effort to get up.

Rock retained enough composure to know that Mollie could not survive in the water with Maude holding her down. He tried with all his might to unhook Maude from the wagon quickly so she could get up. He hoped this would free Mollie, but Maude's single-tree had jammed so deeply into the mud that he could not reach the chains to unhook them. All of his efforts to free the mules proved futile.

The boy could not hold back his tears as he helplessly watched Mollie, his favorite mule, struggle with all her might to get up, only to fall back under the weight of Maude. The bodies of the two large animals significantly blocked the creek-bed, and the rapidly rising water added to the severity of his problems. He was frantic and helpless as he was compelled to watch Mollie, whom he considered almost a member of the family, drown convulsively right before his eyes.

Maude continued her efforts to get up, and soon pulled her singletree out of the mud so Rock could unhook her from the wagon. He hurried home and made his tearful report to the family. Everyone tried to console the boy and tell him it was not his fault. However, they all agreed there was no way the family could make that crop without Mollie, and there were no funds or credit to buy a new mule. The family situation looked hopeless.

A few days later, the entire New Hope Baptist Church congregation surprised the family by getting together after Sunday morning worship and coming for dinner at the Notleks' home entirely unannounced. Thankfully, they brought dinner with them, and spread it on tables in the side yard where the Church members fellowshipped together.

As the children began their after-meal play, Rev. Johnson slipped out to the family's barn and led out the best looking, most high-spirited horse Rock had seen in a long time. He was a high-stepping, fast-paced, beautiful creature, the likes of which had never graced this family's farm. Newton had always considered horses a luxury they could not afford, but God had answered the family's many prayers in a way the likes of which they could never have dreamed. However, the horse was only on loan for the remainder of the crop year with an option to buy the handsome steed at the end of the year. Nevertheless, he filled the gap in the family's work force in a time of great need.

Rock had only seen his Daddy cry once in his lifetime. Those were tears of grief that came on a morning when Newton had been ill and unable to work for quite a long time. He was mixing leftover black-eyed peas with flour and making patties to fry for the family's breakfast when he broke into tears because he could not provide better fare for them.

The second eruption of tears came as he was presented the reins to the beautiful steed. However, his tears at this time were tears of great joy.

Just as soon as the corn crop in the bottomlands was gathered and sold, the family began in mid-August to plow the bottom land again, for what they knew to be a terrific gamble. They would plant the entire twelve acres in pole beans that would be ready for market in late October. If this crop happened to be successful, there would not be many farms in the whole state of Georgia with that particular product at that late season of the year, and the price should be top dollar. With hopes running high, they laid out the rows and added fertilizer over the entire field.

The planted seed soon sprouted and Rock could envision Santa Claus with a full sack for that year. As the plants began to put on runners, the boy came to realize that a part of the nefarious plan for that bean crop called for him and Uncle Pitt to go to a nearby swampy cane-break and cut thousands upon thousands of small canes, trim off all their foliage and carry them to the bean patch. The sharpened butts of these canes were then thrust into the ground about six to eight inches deep and each pole-bean runner trained up its individual cane (or pole—hence the name). It was back breaking labor, but they finally brought it to completion.

The beans began to mature and a few of them were ready for market in late October. The family searched for and picked each individual bean as it matured and carried the first load to the produce wholesale buyer for a chain of grocery stores. He was elated with the quality of their product and promised to buy every bean the family could supply at the phenomenal price of three dollars a bushel. His purchase of the first batch of beans paid all of the family's expenses for seed and fertilizer for the entire crop. Now, they could look forward to real profit. It seemed to Rock, who never looked forward to work, that Monday would never come so the family could get back into the field to pick those precious beans that had matured over the weekend.

Monday's harvest never came. Instead, a huge killing frost, unexpected that early in the year in their part of Georgia, came on Sunday night and made every bean in the field unsuitable for market. Frostbitten beans cannot even be canned for personal use. It was the last straw for the family's life on the farm. Newton and Rosa began their plans to move their family back to the city.

They rented a house in East Point quite near Russell High School where most of the family members who remained at home were students, or soon would become students. Rock took great delight in the fact that he could now walk to school, and even greater delight that he could come home for lunch and could eat as much as he wanted.

A ROLLING ROCK GATHERS NO MOSS

LIFE IN THE CITY presented a new and strange set of situations for the redhead. He no longer faced the dreaded bus ride that lasted for more than an hour early every morning and even longer in the afternoon because he had to wait at Sandtown School while the bus took the students home who lived on its northern route. He could walk to or from school in less than ten minutes from the new location. In spite of these blessings, he continued to have a great longing for his pack of Beagle hounds he had to give away as the family moved from the farm.

"Jimmy," the boy said to his brother, "I'm glad I don't have to milk those old cows every morning any more, or look after any chickens, or hitch up an old mule after school. But I'd be glad to do every bit of that again just to be able to hear old Betsy and Katie and Bud run a rabbit through the woods every afternoon when I come home from school. By the way, you'd better be glad you're working up at Fort Mac and get home too late to have to work in the garden.

"You would not believe how much work Daddy can make you put into a little old garden spot that ain't no bigger than 75feet by 200 feet. Man, that little place takes nearly as much of my work time as a 15 acre farm used to take. Maybe I was too hard on old Blackie after all. I sure know now that it ain't no fun havin' to work like a mule."

James had found a great job working for the government at Fort McPherson where he packed and/or unpacked the belongings of Army officers and their families who were moving. The War Department had given all of the armed forces branches a challenge to realign their forces to be ready for rapid deployment in the war that now appeared to be inevitable. This challenge called for much more troop movement than had ever been the case before and, for this reason, James worked overtime on most days. That forced most of the outside duties and the garden chores to be the boy's responsibility.

Thankfully, his morning activities began later than when he had lived in the country, but the waking hours in the evening stretched much later into the hours of darkness. It did not take Rock long to discover his natural tendency to be a night owl, now that electric lights illuminated the family's rented home and other wonders of the electrical age blessed those premises—especially a dependable radio.

When he finally turned 14 and secured a part-time job at the local Big Star Grocery Store, the pressure on his time became progressively greater. School work continued at its steadily increasing pace and required more study time than the boy really wanted to invest in that area. However, he did take his ROTC work quite seriously because he frequently fantasized himself as a soldier winning battles against Hitler's forces. How he hated those Nazis who had begun an invasive sweep through the continent of Europe.

The boy paid very close attention to the local instructor of his ROTC unit. Every word that came out of Sgt. Rathiewicz' mouth now gained a new sense of importance and was insatiably absorbed and stored in the memory bank of the avid young pretend warrior. This seriousness about absorbing knowledge soon spread to other areas of his learning experience.

The boy learned in Mr. Cyrus Maddox's math class how to think with progressive logic as he sought answers to math questions. He imagined himself as a detective and the figures given in the problem as his clues in the case. The answer to the problem then became his sought-after criminal. Learning finally became exciting for the redhead because a proper answer to a problem now came to represent a "case closed" stamp for that particular crime.

As he advanced to Geometry, Rock learned to use theorems and axioms as a method of guiding his thought process, and he learned to apply them even in some situations where mathematical figures are not applicable to the problem. Without realizing the full value of his experience, the boy had finally gained the needed tools that would eventually make him a much deeper and more independent thinker and, therefore, a better student.

At about the same time, he had the good fortune of enrolling in the English class taught by Miss Lois Parr, whose distinct pronunciations and feigned English accent caught the redhead's attention almost immediately. Under her tutelage, he learned the importance of proper diction, as well as different usages and double entendre possibilities of our language that could make for wonderful word-games and banter for fun. A completely new world of conversation began to open for the excited student.

His baptism in the fire of the dead language, Latin, soon reinforced this excitement. Under the watchful eye of Miss Virginia Moody, he learned to recognize word-roots based on Latin. With this knowledge, many previously strange words became meaningful to and useful for the boy. This increased his spoken vocabulary considerably and absolutely exploded his reading comprehension.

Now that the boy had these academic tools under his belt, he felt more adequately prepared to face the rigors of the higher education process he must follow if he would ever become a medical missionary. By this time, he was nearly ready for his senior high school year. How he wished he had completed this study background before he so nearly tripped over *The Ancient Mariner* and *Julius Caesar* during that freshman English course.

His job at the Big Star store became more and more demanding of his time and left less time to devote to his studies. At the end of each pay period, he would dutifully hand over his unopened pay envelope to his mother. She doled back a minimum amount of money to the boy, but only enough to pay for food at those times when he could not ride his bicycle home for lunch. Every dollar of the money he earned appeared to be necessary to help the family with living expenses. No funds remained that his mother could put aside for his college education. So the boy worried and his self-esteem dropped another notch.

Three heart-warming but unexpected surprises came for the redhead near the end of his junior year. These instances of recognition put new vigor into his resolve to reach the goals he had set for his life and to continue his push for knowledge. First, he was selected as a member by the Russell High chapter of the National Honor Society.

"Gosh," he said when he heard this good news, "I thought those bad grades in freshman English had blown that ship completely out of the water."

He could not contain his nervous excitement as he entered the restaurant on the night of his initiation into the Honor Society. It was his first time ever to experience a "high-class" restaurant where he would sit and have someone serve him. His Mother versed him as well as she knew about the things that represented good manners, but he feared some of the habits developed at a family table often crowded with 12 or more people might spill over into his actions that night. He watched other people closely and nervously to see how they handled themselves in every aspect of this situation. It gave him some sense of relief when he realized that most of them were watching others and were equally as uncertain about how to act.

Where do I place the napkin? Which fork do I use and for what food? Rock wrestled with these questions as did many of the new Honor Society members. However, George, who was President of the Honor Society, seemed at perfect ease about how to conduct himself in the situation. Finally, every eye fell on him and he put everyone else at ease when the waiter asked him, "What type of steak sauce would you like, Sir?"

George replied, "Well, as tough as my steak is, I would think shoe-polish might be the best selection."

A second surprise came when Miss Moody approached him and said, "Rock, I want you to represent Russell High School in the annual Fulton County Latin contest."

The immediate reply of the startled boy came with an excuse, "Miss Moody, I appreciate your asking me, but you know how busy I am. I won't have time enough to review and study all that stuff for a test like that and still work as much as I have to work every day after school."

"Oh, Rock," Miss Moody chided, "you're not fooling me one bit. I know you haven't really been studying for my classes until after you come into the classroom. You're just a natural at Latin, and I think you're the best Latin student in the county without even trying hard. It will fool me if you don't win the contest. It will not take much of your time just to take a simple test."

The boy agreed to enter the contest and even went so far as to review some of the Latin rules and a few of its declensions. When time came for the contest, he sat ready in his place. The test monitor placed the papers face down on each contestant's desk. At the appointed time, the monitor gave the order for each contestant to turn over his test paper and begin. No one had permission to ask any questions of the test monitor, who might not be a Latin teacher and might not have real knowledge of the language.

The fact that the test appeared so easy really shocked the boy. He did find what he considered a typographical error in the test. It called for the pluperfect declension of a certain verb. He had never heard the word "pluperfect" before that time, but felt assured it called for the plural perfect of the verb. He recorded that declension on his test paper, finished the test well before time expired and left for work.

About two weeks later, a tearful Virginia Moody pulled the boy aside as he entered Latin class. "Rock," she said through her tears, "you placed second in the Fulton County Latin contest. The only error you made in the entire test was to give the plural perfect where they asked for the pluperfect declension—and that's my fault.

"The pluperfect is what I consider to be a rogue term for the past perfect, and I have never used that word in teaching Latin. I even chose a textbook for this class that does not include the term. If I had only told you about it, you would have had a perfect paper. It is my fault that you are not the champion Latin student for all of Fulton County."

"Don't worry about it Miss Moody," said the boy with a shrug of his shoulders as he took his seat in the classroom and looked for the first time at his Latin lesson for the day. *No skin off my shoulder*, he mused. *I just got into her old contest to please Miss Moody, and now I've made her cry because I didn't win. Well, I did the best I could do. It ain't my fault.* He shed not one tear over his near miss in the contest, and that was unusual for the redhead.

The third surprise came when tough ROTC instructor, Sgt. Rathiewicz, commissioned Rock as a Captain in the ROTC unit before the boy had reached the age of 15. This meant he could begin to wear one of those great looking officer's dress uniforms and even carry a sword and scabbard, a thing he had actually fantasized about only a few months earlier. In addition, he would soon have a part in the military honor guard's arch of swords the graduating seniors would march ceremoniously under as they proceeded to the stage for the graduation exercise.

All-in-all, it proved to be an excellent time in the boy's life. These three unexpected honors were the first steps in a process that began raising his level of self-esteem from its previous level of negative twenty.

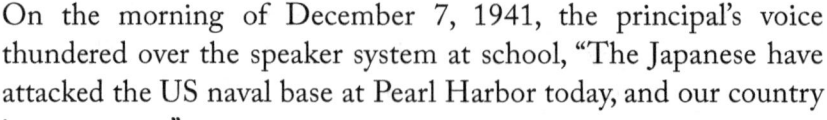

On the morning of December 7, 1941, the principal's voice thundered over the speaker system at school, "The Japanese have attacked the US naval base at Pearl Harbor today, and our country is now at war."

Rock was a senior in high school when his beloved America made this declaration. This gave much more purpose to his ROTC training and caused him to apply even greater diligence to the training of the fledgling soldiers in his ragtag company of freshman students.

Wartime brought many changes in every life in the USA. Rock's Daddy became a volunteer air-raid warden. Many women took jobs previously reserved for men only. Multitudes of men volunteered for military service, while their draft boards called up even more. Rationing of many food items now became a fact of life for everyone…red stamps for meat, blue for canned or dried vegetables or fruits, and special stamps for coffee and sugar. The government also rationed gasoline, tires, shoes and many other items including nylon stockings.

For the redhead, the change showed most profoundly in his job at the Big Star grocery Store where he gained a promotion from being a lowly bag-boy. His task now consisted of taking the customers' purchases from the shopping carts and placing them on the checkout counter. As he placed the items on the counter, using only his wits, he had to add up each type of required ration stamp, keeping each color separate. Then he must collect the stamps and return any overpayment of points to the customer before the cash register operator was ready to collect the money for those purchases. It was not an easy task, but Rock was glad to have a small part in our war effort. And, after all, they did raise his pay from a quarter to thirty-five cents an hour.

Things did not seem all that bad on the home front for the boy except for a few occasions when someone passing by looked at his large frame and yelled obscenities loudly enough for everyone to hear, "Hey, you %&@* draft dodger. Why in the %#*^ ain't you in the army?"

That made the redhead's patriotic blood boil because he could not join any branch of the service at age 15, and he was doing all he knew to do for the war effort. He kept his mouth shut and did his job.

On the night of his graduation from high school, Newton pulled the boy aside and told him frankly, "Son, you can be anything you want to be…and can afford to be." Rock knew that meant his father stood behind him in his endeavor but could not bear any of the expense of his further education.

At the graduation exercise, he received another unexpected honor in the form of a small scholarship from Mercer University in Macon, Georgia. The operative word here proved to be "small," in that the scholarship only paid $33.00 per quarter for the first two quarters of his freshman year and $34.00 in the third quarter. It stood valueless after the freshman year. At least it represented a symbolic start, being the first dime available for his further education.

Then, later that night, his Mother made a promise to her son, "Rock, if you will work all you can at the Big Star this summer, I promise you I will put up every dime I can possibly save from it for your college education."

Buoyed by that promise, the redhead worked every hour the store would allow and still turned his unopened pay envelope over to his Mother each week. He did not worry excessively about the money, because James had promised to help some in his support while the boy attended school. Of course, he knew he would need to find work to supplement those family contributions.

Being a high school graduate made Rock even more painfully aware of his own immaturity. The fact that he could not even drive a car was a constant source of embarrassment, and he would soon be sixteen. When church services dismissed on Sunday after his graduation, the family returned to their car and found the redhead sitting in the driver's seat. "Please let me drive, Mother. After all, I am a high school graduate, and am nearly sixteen now. Surely, I have earned some rights."

At first, his Mother resisted but she finally relented as the boy's pleas persisted, "Okay, Son, since you put it that way, I'll let you drive. But be careful and don't you dare to drive fast."

"I promise, Mother," said the boy as he cranked the car and finally ground the gears until he located first gear. The heavy car jerked and bumped the half block down the street to the first corner. He grinned as he successfully made a right turn after a proper hand signal. Then panic set in when he spotted an oncoming car speeding down his side of the street and headed directly toward them. The boy jerked the steering wheel to the right. The next thing he knew, the car jumped onto the sidewalk and hit a power pole leaving it completely severed near its base and swinging freely from its wires. Thankfully, no one had any injuries and there appeared to be not a scratch or dent on the old car. However, all of the positive effects the recent good events had on the boy's ego now faded into the past as he blurted out, "I'll never try to drive again as long as I live."

The summer ended and time for the boy's college entrance arrived. Along with it came two blows to his college funding. James decided that he must also go to college to fulfill his own calling which, by this time, had dropped the missionary aspect. He would join Rock in enrolling at Mercer as a ministerial student. Secondly, when his Mother doled out his money from the entire summer's work, it amounted to a measly $25.00. It took a lot of faith (or should one call it ignorance?) for a 16 year old to go off to college with no job, no promise of a job, and only a hundred dollar scholarship plus $25 cash in his pocket.

His ignorance showed itself in greater abundance during the boy's college admission interview. Despite the fact that his older brother stood by his side, he was very nervous as the interviewer began. "Mr. Notleks,—"

Rock acted startled because no one had ever called him "Mr." before,—"what degree do you want to pursue at Mercer?"

"An MD degree," replied the redhead, ignorant of the fact he would have to earn a basic degree before he could even begin to study medicine.

"No. I mean what degree do you wish to pursue here at Mercer?" replied the interviewer.

"An MD degree, I told you," replied the redhead, trying not to let his impatience show.

"No, Mr. Notleks. Apparently you do not understand. You cannot get an MD degree at Mercer."

"Do you mean that after traveling at least a hundred miles, the farthest I've ever been from home, I'm at the wrong place? I have this scholarship paper right here that Mercer gave me, and they know I came here to study to be a doctor.

"You see, I had this calling to be a medical missionary when I was plowing in the peanut patch one day. It didn't come as dramatically as Moses' calling came with the burning bush and all that kind of stuff, but I still had this calling…You are a Baptist, ain't you? And you do believe in callings, don't you?"

"Yes, Mr. Notleks, I do believe in callings, but you obviously do not understand the process. I will try to explain it to you. You can begin your study toward an MD degree here at Mercer, and the first step is to complete a premedical course of study that will gain you either an AB or a BS degree. After that, you must go to a medical school somewhere and study for your MD degree. That will take four more years, and then you will become an intern. After a year or so as an intern, you will then become a full-fledged doctor."

The boy could not help but think, *all of those degrees sound like a lot of BS to me and I feel just like I'm gettin' the third degree*. However, he replied simply, "It's a good thing I'm gettin' an early start. Sounds like a feller could easily get to be an old man before he ever gets a chance to be a doctor. No wonder they've all got gray hair."

Finally, the redhead saw the big picture and realized the enormity of the task before him. He thought to himself, *it is probably a good thing I didn't know how long it would take. I never would have had the nerve to strike out on a ten year project with what little money I have in my pocket right now. I guess God kept me dumb for a reason…and I thought we had some long rows to hoe when I worked on the farm*…his thoughts trailed off.

Now officially enrolled as a premedical student at Mercer, Rock was disappointed to learn that his scholarship came with a price tag. To pay for the grant, he had to act as a chapel monitor and report anyone who had an assigned seat in his section of the chapel and missed any of those required sessions.

"Jimmy, I hate having to do what they are making me do. It makes me feel like a little tattletale snitch back in grammar school. If I report everyone who misses their old chapel services, I won't have even one friend in my chapel section by the end of this year. I wish they hadn't even given me their old scholarship," he complained, knowing full well the last part of his statement contained a lie.

James had some business experience, so he acted as agent for the two brothers in all matters. He found several menial tasks for them to do on campus to help pay their tuition. Those jobs included tasks like rolling and lining off clay tennis courts and sweeping the gymnasium after varsity basketball games. The two boys and their new friend, Earl Queen, also washed dishes three times a day, five days a week for 100 male students. When James got an evening job in sales at a local military supply and luggage store, it left the redhead to do most of the evening dishes. Naturally, he complained, "Gosh, Jimmy. It looks as if Earl could do more than he does, but I guess he figures he just agreed to do one-third of the work."

Of course, the boy worked every Friday afternoon and all day on Saturday at the Big Star grocery store in Macon, logging at least 20 hours in those two days. He netted about seven dollars for these efforts before the relatively new Social Security Administration took their deduction.

Near the end of their freshman year, James signed the redhead up for the night watchman's job on campus. In this position, he made rounds seven nights a week at hourly intervals beginning at 10 p.m. and ending just as soon as he could complete the 1 a.m. rounds. This brought the weekly total of hours Rock worked to about 65. Add that to the 20 quarter hours of college academic courses along with PE and laboratory time extra, it did not leave much time for study…but it did pay the tuition.

As night watchman, the boy's duty was to look for and report any evidence of fire or other dangerous situations, and to report any suspicious activities on the campus. No one ever gave him any instructions as to what action he should take on the occasional occurrence when he found a couple of students in some rather compromising positions in various parts of the campus.

Naturally, the surprised students tried to hide their faces as they scurried from the scene, but the young night watchman had already seen their faces and recognized them. He knew every person who belonged on Mercer's small campus. Wisely, he refrained from reporting to anyone the juicy details he sometimes witnessed and he gained the respect of many rather sheepish fellow students in the process.

It did enter his mind that blackmail could possibly pay a portion of his tuition, but he knew he could never stoop that low. In his mind, he calculated that he had made more loyal and devoted friends because of his silence in these night matters than he had ever gained by his selective blindness as a chapel monitor. *They say silence is golden,* he thought each time he met one of these students on campus, *but my silence has never brought any gold to me.*

As night watchman, the boy carried a punch clock in a heavy leather case that hung by a strap over his shoulder. At each of the five different locations on the campus, he picked up a key that nestled in a metal box mounted on a wall and inserted it into the clock to verify his presence at that station at the required time. One of these stations lurked behind the girl's dormitory in an outside stairwell leading to a basement door. That station required the boy to visit a spot where he felt very uncomfortable.

To reach the checkpoint, he had to cross an elevated walkway that led to the girl's dining hall. This meant he had to climb three or four marble steps up to the walkway, then down the corresponding steps on the far side, cross a courtyard and a second elevated walkway. He would then make a 180 degree turn and go down the outside stairs to the station where he punched his clock.

In the rounds he made before midnight, the boy utilized the time on his rounds to try to increase the range of his singing voice. As he rapidly walked across the campus, he could often be heard singing scales or selected songs trying to reach higher or lower notes than he had ever been able to reach before, yet attempting to retain his voice quality.

His rounds at 1 a.m. were an entirely different matter. There was no time wasted in walking and there was no singing. Knowing he could go to sleep as soon as he completed this round, the boy developed a technique of running the entire cycle around the campus. He picked up his clock in the boiler room and punched that station at one on the dot. He then bolted out the door and across the truckers' delivery area where he took a flying leap into the dark and landed near the bottom of the eight-foot embankment alongside the campus laundry building.

From that point he rushed to the Co-op to punch station# 2, then high-tailed across the street to the rear of the girls dormitory where he darted at maximum speed across the lawn to the elevated walkway. He jumped in one single bound on to the center of the walkway and, with a second bound, into the courtyard. Then he sped across the courtyard and the second walkway, and down the stairwell to his key-station. From there, he puffed uphill to the Ad building, the Willingham Chapel and back to the boiler room from where he scurried to his bed in the gymnasium basement.

On one particularly memorable night, the flying freshman literally leaped into an embarrassing situation as he bounded into the courtyard of the girls dorm at about 1:05 a.m. When the boy finally dragged to his room that night well after 1:30 a.m., Jimmy shouted at him, "Rock, where in this world have you been? I have been worried sick about you. I had already gotten up to get dressed and come look for you."

"You won't believe me when I tell you," moaned the redhead.

"Try me and see," retorted his older brother.

"Well, you see, Jimmy, it was like this. You know how much I hurry on those last rounds so I can get to sleep a little bit earlier."

"Yes, yes, I know."

"Well, tonight when I came bustin' around the corner of the girls' dormitory, that place was lighted up like they were having a football game. Anyhow, the girls had all the windows open and a whole lot of them were sitting in the windows with their backsides sticking out into the courtyard. I don't know, but I figure the Dean of Women must have had an idea that some of her girls had slipped out of the dormitory and she had called them all together to try and find what was going on."

"Really?" questioned James, showing both interest and amazement. "Then what happened?"

"Those girls started screaming and hollering when I bounded over the dining room walkway and sprang like gang-busters into the court yard. Every one of them jumped down from the windows and scattered into the parlor and the front hall. I could hear Dean Wardlaw yelling out directions and trying to calm them down," the redhead continued.

"What did you do, Rock?"

"I didn't know what to do. I was running so fast, there was no way I could stop—and besides—I'd already scared the bejeebers out of them. I felt pretty sure none of them had recognized me, as fast as I was going, so I wasn't about to stop and introduce myself. I just bounced right on down to my clock station and I didn't move a single muscle except to breathe for quite a while," Rock whimpered in a half whisper, just beginning to recover a small amount of composure.

"And then?" prodded his older brother.

"The girls finally settled down a little and I could hear Dean Wardlaw talking to the police about an intruder or a peeping tom or something like that. Man, I knew I didn't want to stay there and have those guys come and find me hiding in that stairwell, so I just crept up the stairs and finished my rounds. It seemed like I would never get back here to the room."

"It sounds like you handled the situation pretty well for a sixteen-year-old boy. I'm proud of you, Rock." Jimmy's words of praise reverberated in the boy's ears like the music of a chorus of angels.

The freshman year finally dragged to its completion and the boy could hardly believe it had only been nine months—it felt so much longer. One of the reasons it seemed so long came from the fact that the University had to disband his beloved Glee Club, his one avocation, after the first quarter when its director moved and no one was available to fill his place.

Rock felt tired from all the hours of work and study, but he had maintained his grades at a relatively high average and, between the two boys, they had managed to pay all of their tuition. However, he had completely drained his miniscule financial reserves and, even though its amount had been paltry, he had to face the fact that he would not have his scholarship any longer. He talked it over with his brother and together they decided their best course would be to go home for the summer and save every penny they could possibly spare to be ready for September, 1943, and a new year at college.

The new school year brought a new and unexpected challenge for the redhead. A mere two weeks before leaving for the University, he learned that not only would James accompany him to Mercer, but his two older sisters, Rosa and Helen, would also enroll as students there. The quartet of students would rent one of the ancient duplex apartments that stood in a line along the street most students affectionately referred to as "Poverty Row." The University owned these units and usually reserved them for married ministerial students and their families. This represented quite a departure from the average person's college life, but the boy had not really had the average experience during his first year in college and he welcomed this experiment as well.

The beginning of the boy's sophomore college year was literally a moving experience for all four of the siblings. Their beds and dressers, plus their cooking utensils, silverware and dishes along with a few precious staple groceries—in fact, all of the items needed to set up full housekeeping—were included in the cargo of the entourage that headed out for Mercer on that bright end-of-summer day. Although it was not a new thing, having only one bathroom in their duplex apartment on Poverty Row became a real bone of contention when four students were getting ready for eight a.m. classes. After all, one bathroom had sufficed for the full family of eight ever since they had moved to a house that boasted any type of indoor plumbing facilities.

The bathroom matter deserved only a minor degree of attention compared to the necessity now of earning tuition, books, rent and food for four college students, with the gluttonous Rock being one of them. Having pooled all of the family resources at the start, the group barely had enough money for about half of the first quarter's tuition and the house rent for the first month, but they did bring a relatively large larder of food from home with them. From that point on, it became a venture of faith.

James was welcomed back at his job from the previous year at the luggage and military supply store; and he secured a job alongside him for Helen. Rosa served as the housekeeper and cook for the four students and she found a two hour a day job at the campus post office. Rock had turned seventeen and met the requirements for employment at the store with James and Helen. This made a tremendous difference in his life. Now he could work only 40 or so hours per week and bring in more money than he had earned in his previous 65 hour per week expenditure of time. This meant he had a little time he could spare for extracurricular activities.

One drastic change had taken place during the boys' three-month absence from school. A large number of students who wore uniforms of the US Navy had invaded the campus. The war was in high gear and things were not yet going as well as desired for the US armed forces around the world. Therefore, the highest echelons in Washington had made a decision to use the existing colleges as areas to educate leaders and needed professionals (physicists, chemists, doctors and lawyers) for the war effort, and to teach needed basic sciences to aspiring aviators.

The major purpose of the Navy V-5 unit that existed at Mercer was to prepare young sailors for entry into naval aviation, but there were a few in the V-12 program designed to prepare them for professional schools including medical schools. The presence of these students set the redhead to thinking.

It won't be long before I become 18 and eligible for the draft. Perhaps I can join the V-12 before my draft date, and let them pay my tuition for medical school. People tell me there is no way a person can work his way through that difficult program unless he already has a Ph.D. and can teach somewhere in the university system.

His scheming went even further as he thought; *I still have nearly a year of premedical studies ahead of me. Before I join the V-12, if I take only those subjects I am required to take as a premedical student, I will not have enough hours to get a college degree before I go to medical school. On the other hand, if I take enough electives before I join, then my required courses will give me enough credits for my degree.* Based on this thinking, his course was set for the rest of his college career.

For the first time in his academic career, the boy began to take a few elective courses along with the required courses for premedical study, and he looked forward to the time when he could apply for the V-12 program. He took great comfort in the fact that at last he could see clearly what path God had chosen to defray the huge costs of his medical education. In his mind now, it became just a matter of time.

The date finally arrived for him to take the written examination for appointment to the V-12 program and, as he frequently did, he slept through his alarm that morning. When he arrived breathless at the examination site, his greeting from the officer in charge was anything but friendly. "Notleks," he said, "you're late. If you had been just one minute later, I would not have let you in. Don't think you will get any extra time for this test. You chose to get a late start, but I choose the ending time. Your paper will be handed in at the same time as the rest."

"Yes, Sir, I'm sorry, but my alarm did not wake me up, Sir," said the boy, determined to do well on the test in spite of his tardiness.

After all, God had charted this course for him. He took his paper, found a seat and went to work. Time did not become a factor for him and he even had time to check every answer on his paper before he handed it in when the bell rang.

Waiting for the letter from the Department of the Navy about his test score proved very hard for the boy. Every day seemed like a week and he became more and more nervous. When the letter finally did arrive, it made no mention of his score, but it did enclose an appointment for a pre-admission physical examination.

"I'm in," the boy shouted to his family. "All I have to do now is to pass their old physical examination, and I certainly don't have any worries about that."

Again, time seemed to pass very slowly before the physical examination came due, and the boy's impatience showed at times. "Why does it take so long?" he asked his brother.

"Rock," retorted Jimmy, "when I worked at Fort McPherson, I learned that anything the government is involved with just naturally takes a long time. Just hold on and be patient. It will come in its own time."

The date for his scheduled physical examination finally arrived and, on this occasion, the boy made certain he made his appearance with plenty of time to spare. He did have a little apprehension about the examination itself. He had never undergone a physical examination of any type except for the time when he almost had his appendix removed, and he did not know what to expect. He certainly did not like the idea of parading about in front of all those people without wearing any clothes. Nevertheless, the boy breezed through every examining station without any adverse comment from any doctor and, presumably, had passed with flying colors.

The Genito-Urinary check was the final station he had to endure in his examination and the doctor had completely missed the redhead's congenital deformity. As the Urologist began writing his report, the still naked boy turned his deformed organ up to plain view of the doctor and asked his examiner, "Did you ever see anything like that?"

The Urologist gasped and grabbed a ruler from his desk to measure how far back the urethral aperture lay from the organ' stip. With a gesture of helplessness, he said the saddest two words the redhead had ever heard, "That's disqualifying."

Rock actually thought he would die on the spot and he could not restrain his tears as he put on his clothes for the lonely trip home. It seemed to him his entire world had crashed before him as he muttered, "And I was so certain that was God's plan for me... but I can't quit now. I have too much invested. Something is bound to turn up."

In the meantime, Mercer secured a new Professor of Music. One of Dr. Rich's first actions was to form a male double quartet because he claimed such a small group could get off the ground faster and represent the University in the community much more quickly than a larger group. He asked Rock to be a charter member of this octet, selecting him as one of the first tenors. This gave the boy a chance to do some traveling for their performances. However, their travel had to be greatly limited at the time by the many wartime shortages that were especially critical for tires and gasoline.

About this time, the boy submitted his admission application requests, accompanied by a copy of his college transcript, to both medical schools in the State of Georgia, Emory University School of Medicine and the Medical College of Georgia. Shortly after his filing of the applications, the boy received his acceptance from each of these medical institutions in rapid succession, pending only his successful completion of certain required premedical courses. According to federal law, acceptance to medical school removed any possibility of the government drafting him into military service.

More good news followed that good news. Dr. Rich would reconstitute the Glee Club and, for the first time in recent years, Mercer would also form a Drama Club. The boy could not contain his elation as he spoke to his brother, "I know you're not at all interested in the Drama Club, Jimmy, but I have never had a chance to be in a play since I was in the fifth grade. I couldn't even try out for our senior play in high school because I had to work all the time. I'm going to join both the Glee Club and the Drama Club and see what happens."

After the organizational meeting for the Glee Club, Rock ran home breathlessly. "Jimmy, Jimmy," he called excitedly, "guess what happened."

"I know what happened, Rock," responded his brother. "They elected you president of the Glee Club. Remember, Rosa and Helen were there, too. I'm proud of you, boy. You deserve it."

"Jimmy, when they nominated me for president, I couldn't believe my ears that it was my name they were calling. You could have knocked me over with a feather. No one has ever even nominated me for any office before in all my life…much less elected me to one. And to think I actually am now the president of the Mercer Glee Club. It's hard to believe," the boy said dreamily.

With his new duties as Glee Club president added to his already heavy academic schedule and full time job, the boy had about all he could handle. He had completed almost three academic years of work in a little more than 18 calendar months, and was about to enter his last trimester of premed carrying 21 academic hours with three lab courses. His hectic schedule forced him to take physical education classes along with the Navy trainees, where he was the only civilian in the class.

Because of this heavy workload, he changed his mind about attending the organizational meeting of the Drama Club. At the last moment, however, he decided to go to the meeting and, as he had said, "see what happens." For the second time in a row, he received a nomination to be president of an organization. This time, there were no further nominations for the office and his election came by unanimous vote. The redhead now served as president of two meaningful campus organizations and there is no way to measure the positive effect those honors had on his self-confidence.

The Drama Club busied itself—not with discussion of what work to perform—but with discussion of all the details of obtaining equipment and personnel to assist in a stage production of any sort. This did not prove to be an easy task during a time of war shortages in a strapped for cash university where there had not been such a program for many years. However, the club members pursued their goals with the vigor of youth and under the guidance of a young faculty advisor. Progress was agonizingly slow.

The Glee Club's progress was an entirely different matter. Dr. Rich brought all of the know-how for its organization and operation, and the University still had sufficient space, materials and music for the Glee Club to begin practice immediately. That organization succeeded in being up and running very quickly just by opening its doors; and the talent pool among the students truly was amazing. To everyone's surprise, Dr. Rich chose to begin the schedule of public performances for the group with one of the world's most difficult works, Handel's Messiah. Much work lay ahead before the glee club could polish this undertaking enough for its performance.

In the meantime, Rock had met a girl at Glee Club practice. Nancy's shoulder length, flowing, black hair that stood in stark but wonderful contrast to her delicate white skin greatly impressed the boy. He even got up the nerve to walk across the campus with her on several different occasions and, once or twice, he held her hand in the process. The boy thought he might be falling in love, and things seemed to be going well in his life.

Rock was riding high and felt almost invincible when the unexpected phone call came from his mother. Long distance phone calls were quite expensive and members of Rock's family never used them except in times of genuine emergency. A long-distant call usually signaled a problem and as he said, "Hello," his voice trembled slightly with fear.

"Rock, this is Mother," the excited sounding voice came over the phone. "In this morning's mail, you got a note from the draft board giving you a ten day notice before you must report for military service."

"Oh, that's okay, Mother. Don't worry one bit about it," responded the boy with a great sigh of relief. "You know the law says that I'm not eligible to be drafted since I have been accepted to medical school."

"I know that, son, but I am worried. I called the draft board this morning. They mentioned that none of the Notleks boys have ever served in this war and they did not think that was right. Daddy and I plan to appear before them in the morning and see what we can work out."

"That's a good idea, Mother. Be sure to tell them I have letters from two medical schools informing me that I am accepted. All I have to do is complete this trimester's courses with satisfactory grades, and I have already enrolled in those courses and am getting good grades. That should be all the information you will need to get those guys off our backs."

The phone call the following day did not alarm the boy, who felt certain it brought a report from the draft board meeting. "What did the draft board have to say, Mother?" he asked with great interest.

"Well, son, they promised to give you a 30 day delay of your induction to give us time to get those letters to them, but they would not put that promise into writing. I'm still worried because I don't feel we can trust that bunch down there. Remember, they have already made some snide comments about none of you boys ever being in the service," responded his mother.

"Aw, Mother, you worry too much. We have thirty days and I'm planning to come home in two weeks. I can bring the papers then. That still leaves us two weeks to get the papers in their hands," said the boy as he went back to his duties.

Not quite a week later, his Mother's third long distance call within less than ten days did alarm the boy. It came after four p.m., and his Mother sounded excited and unhappy. "Rock," she said, "the draft board just called and said you must report to Fort McPherson by no later than eight o'clock tomorrow morning to be inducted into the army. I told you they were up to no good when they wouldn't put it in writing about delaying your induction. I don't see anything for you to do other than catch the next bus and come home. I'll have your bed made and your supper ready at whatever time you get here.

At that late hour, the registrar's office at the University had already closed, so the boy could not officially withdraw from school before he left. He did not even have time to tell Nancy good-bye. He caught the next bus that left for home, knowing he would have to notify the school by mail of his call to active duty in the US Army.

His country had called him and, even though he felt his draft board had not acted correctly, he would answer its call without question or complaint. If he passed the physical examination for the Army, he would serve his country to the best of his ability.

A ROCK-SOLID SOLDIER

A FEW MINUTES BEFORE eight the following morning, the bewildered boy reported to the army base at Fort McPherson in Atlanta to begin his military duty. At this examination facility, the number of men parading naked as they waited their turn to enter each of the specialty examination stations numbered about fifty times as many as on his previous examination for the V-12. Therefore, a sense of anonymity gradually came over the redhead and his discomfort about his public pubic exposure diminished. At the Genito-Urinary section, the boy pointedly demonstrated his deformity to the examining physician and could not help but grin at the doctor's humorous response, "You are not required to do hand-stands and balancing acts on that thing, soldier. Go right ahead and don't hold up the line. You're in the army, now."

The swearing in ceremony came early in the afternoon that day. When Rock, along with hundreds of others, gave his oath of allegiance to his country and his promise to defend her against all enemies, there was no feeling of anonymity. He meant it with all his heart. Shortly after noon the following day, he boarded a train for the first railroad trip of his life.

As fast as that steam locomotive could take them, he and his new fellow recruits headed south. It was the boy's first time ever to leave the State of Georgia, and it represented quite an adventure for him. About midway of the prolonged trip, he learned of his assignment to the infantry and that the group's training destination was Camp Blanding, Florida.

As soon as he arrived at Camp Blanding, he met his new platoon leader, Sgt. Robbins from Puerto Rico. From the very beginning, the Sergeant seemed to like the redhead, partly because the boy already had a significant amount of military knowledge gained from his days in high school ROTC. He made the boy squad leader of the third squad in his platoon. In spite of this show of respect by Sgt. Robbins, there were frequent confrontations between the two when the boy failed to get out of bed the very first time the sergeant blew his whistle.

Each time the stubby Puerto Rican returned to check the barracks and found the derelict redhead still in slumber, he would turn the boy's bed on its side and dump him sprawling on the floor. Rock felt assured that people could hear the small sergeant bellow for a full city block as he repeated the old army saying, "Notleks, you had better give your heart to Jesus, because your ass is mine." The boy had to hear that strong admonition many times before Sgt. Robbins' deeper message that sergeants run the world finally penetrated his hard head. He started to get up when the sergeant's first whistle blew.

The redhead's new outfit, the 237th Infantry Training Battalion, had only been in training for three weeks when the war in Europe took a marked turn for the worse. German forces broke through the Allied lines at the infamous Belgian bulge. Times were tense for all of the allied countries, but nowhere could there be any more tenseness than in the 237th. The Battalion immediately went on standby alert for shipment to Europe as replacements, even though their training had been less than one-fourth completed at the time. It brought a new meaning to the word "training." All involved parties breathed a collective sigh of relief when the Allies plugged the gap and the Army lifted the standby order.

Captain Coffman, the Commander of Company B, Rock's company, was said to have been an All-American football player at The University of Tennessee, and was still as tough as any road-kill steak would ever be. The redhead caught Captain Coffman's eye because he had no problem enduring the strenuous conditioning program of Army basic training. After all, he had been in the same type program at Mercer when he took PE with the naval officer candidates.

Captain Coffman had many strict rules, one of which decreed that none of the men in his company would ever get into a fight without the captain's calling the entire company together to see the fight and his being there to referee the action. Otherwise, he would take strict disciplinary action. The boy never dreamed that rule would ever apply to him—but that was before Pvt. Strickenhauser transferred into the training company. Apparently, Strickenhauser disliked the redhead on first sight. Rock had no memory of having ever spoken to or even seen Pvt. Strickenhauser before the newcomer confronted him and said bluntly, "I can beat your ass."

Rock had no desire to fight the soldier and tried to brush him off. "Well, it has been done many times before," he replied. "So even if you did beat my—uh uh—tail, you certainly would not be in any virgin territory and you wouldn't have proved very much." The redhead walked away.

Strickenhauser persisted in his effort to antagonize his chosen opponent. Every time he saw the boy, he egged him on with, "I can beat your ass."

Being redheaded and having the expected hot temperament for people with that color hair, plus being only 18 years of age, the boy could not listen to that kind of challenge many times before he felt Strickenhauser's invitation to combat simply must be accepted. The two soldiers duly notified Captain Coffman of their intentions to settle this matter.

At the time set for the big encounter, all of B Company gathered in the area set aside for the match. The supply sergeant procured

16-ounce gloves for each of the combatants so they could not really hurt one another, and Captain Coffman got out his stop watch. The Captain used a hammer to hit a small bell that served as a makeshift gong and the match promptly began.

Strickenhauser's weight was probably a little more than Rock's 185 pounds. Other than that, the two about equally matched one another in height and reach. Both fighters hurried to the middle of the ring and swung wild rights, but neither of those swings connected. Three rounds went by and neither fighter had landed even one blow that in any way affected the other person. During the one-minute rest between the third and fourth rounds, Rock could not believe how tired his arms felt. He said to himself, "If you don't get this thing finished in this round, old Strickenhauser is going to do exactly what he said he could do. Rock, you don't have enough strength left to go more than one more round."

When the gong sounded for the fourth round, Rock rushed out of his corner and swung a hard, wild "haymaker" right hand. Strickenhauser back-stepped adroitly and the boy missed his target by a wide margin, but he continued to rush forward like a charging bull and swung a hard backhand blow with his right hand that landed directly on Strickenhauser's chin. His challenger staggered and dropped to the ground.

Strickenhauser quickly got to his feet again and appealed to Captain Coffman to call the decisive blow a foul and declare him the winner by default, but the Captain turned a deaf ear. Rock certainly did not know if he had committed a foul. He had never met an opponent in a boxing ring before and did not know the rules. No one had ever told him you could not hit with the white part of the glove, as Strickenhauser claimed. As far as the redhead was concerned, they had settled the important matter when Strickenhauser did not want to fight any more—and that suited the redhead just fine.

Rock made quite a number of friends within his platoon, but he especially enjoyed the company of one particular soldier in the barracks next door. "Slim" Mitchum, from Rockmart, GA., had grown up on a farm in rural Georgia and loved to hunt. He also claimed to be a fellow Baptist and liked to talk about religion. The two spent many hours in friendly conversation about their common interests, especially their hunting dogs and other memories from the farm.

One day when several trainees gathered in a bull session in his barracks, Slim pulled out his billfold. When he did, a picture of his sister, Sara, fell onto his cot. She was a very attractive girl, and there were many wolf whistles at the sight of her photograph. A number of the soldiers, including Rock, said to Slim, "Have her write me."

Much to his surprise, Rock received a letter from Sara several days later. In it, she told the boy how highly Slim had spoken of his redheaded friend and she mentioned how lonely her life had become since the war began. The boy, who had never written anything more than a homemade valentine to any girl before this time, promptly answered her letter.

Sara's reply arrived shortly thereafter and began with the words, "Dearest One." These words caused the boy to entertain some interesting thoughts. *My line must be better than I ever gave it credit for being*, he mused with a smile.

Again, he made a prompt reply and he received Sara's answer a few days later. This time, the boy delayed his reply for a few days. The letter brought a response that said, among other things, "My Darling. I just cannot wait until this war is over. Then there won't be anything between us but clothes."

Wow, the redhead thought, my line must be too good. I'll just have to back off from this thing right away. I'm not ready for anything serious. He never made a response to that letter. However, Sara's letters continued to arrive regularly as she made plans to come see her brother graduate from basic training, and seemed to be formulating plans concerning Rock. The boy tried not to show to his friend, Slim, how much he feared that occasion.

Army life agreed with the redhead, because he had gained 24 pounds since his draft date. He had also received great news from Mercer University saying that the faculty had voted him full credit for all the courses he had begun when the call came for him to go into the Army. All parties agreed that he had sufficiently completed the University requirements and they planned to grant him his AB Degree and graduate him along with his regular class, but in absentia. He would be graduating that month.

On the date and hour of his college class graduation, the red head was excited in more ways than one. He lay flat on his belly at the machine-gun firing range and would pull off a burst of fire as he thought; *We're probably lined up for graduation right now.* With a later rat-a-tat-tat he would think; *I'm walking down the aisle now.* Then, finally, *I'm a college graduate.* It gave him quite a thrill and nobody knew it but himself.

When only about four weeks remained in his basic training, Rock received a notice to appear before Captain Coffman on the double. Naturally, the boy thought something bad had happened as he reported with a sharp salute for his respected Captain. "You wished to see me, Sir?" he questioned.

"Yes, Pvt. Notleks," Captain Coffman commenced, "I want to speak to you about an important matter. I have had my eye on you all the time you've been here in basic training. You appear to be the type of fellow who is not afraid to face whatever is out there, and you seem to make reasonable decisions about how to handle most things. I see by your record where you are already a college graduate even though you are only eighteen, and that you had four years of ROTC when you were in high school. I'm not even going to begin to talk about your IQ score. You might ask about mine.

"I have already filled out the papers for you to apply for Infantry Officer's Candidate School (OCS) at Fort Benning, Georgia. I want you to sign those papers this morning. We need men like you who are tough and smart and dedicated to be platoon leaders for our troops when we go to invade the islands around Japan."

"But, Captain Coffman…" stammered the redhead.

"Don't you 'but' me, Private," snapped the Captain. "When your country needs you to do a certain job, you don't even think of turning your back on that responsibility. I said for you to sign the papers."

Rock could not help but be flattered by the words Captain Coffman had used to describe him. Deep down inside, he still thought of himself as a sniveling cry baby. He did not realize how much he had grown up in such a short time, but his grisly, tough Captain had referred to him as being able to handle tough situations.

"Yes, Sir, Captain Coffman, just as you say, Sir, but I hate to leave my buddies who are heading for combat now." Responded Rock. He immediately signed the papers the captain had placed before him.

The day soon arrived for the boy's appearance for an interview concerning his possible OCS appointment. As he entered the waiting room, he saw a couple of soldiers he knew only casually also waiting for the same type of interview. Naturally, the topic of their conversation quickly became "What do you suppose we will be asked in the interview?" but they could only speculate about that subject.

An officer finally called Rock's name and he nervously entered the conference room where the interview began with only general questions that he could answer easily until they felt certain the boy had settled down. Then the questions got tougher. Finally, one of the Majors on the board asked Rock, "Tell me, Pvt. Notleks, what makes you think you would make a good officer into day's Army?"

The redhead hesitated a bit, and then stammered his reply. "Well, Sir, I think before one can be good at giving orders, he must first know how to receive and follow orders. With the Mother I have, I know quite well how to follow orders, Sir."

The entire panel chuckled a bit and the interview ended as the Major told the boy, "That will be all, Pvt. Notleks. Go back to your barracks."

Rock left the room to return to his barracks. As he passed through the reception area where the other candidates were still awaiting their interviews, they besieged the redhead with questions, mainly, "What did they ask?"

Before he could answer any of their questions, the Major from the interview team burst into the room to call the next soldier for his interview. He yelled at the redhead quite harshly, "Private

Notleks, I thought you said you knew how to follow orders. Didn't I just order you to go back to your barracks? Now do exactly as I ordered and get back to your squad."

Rock slunk from the interview site convinced he would never be an officer in this man's Army after that debacle. However, his orders to report to OCS were received in a very few days and they called for an extension of his stay at Camp Blanding for two more weeks. His decision to go to OCS would cancel the redhead's immediate deployment to the Pacific Theatre of operations where most of those in his training company were going. His emotions about that were certainly mixed, but the words of Captain Coffman when he all but ordered the boy to apply for OCS still rung in his ears, "We need men…like you…" It was his duty to stay and receive further training in OCS.

Rock still had major concern about Slim's sister, Sara, who planned to come to their graduation ceremony. He thought the situation over and reasoned to himself, *Our upcoming graduation exercise probably means a lot more to the rest of my Company than it does to me. I have just been graduated from college and what I am really looking forward to now is my graduation from OCS. Someone has to take care of feeding the troops that day, and I think the proper thing for me to do is to volunteer for KP duty instead of attending the ceremony. That will allow some person to be there that the ceremony would probably have more meaning for them than it would have for me.*

His true reason finally emerged when he admitted in his thoughts aloud, "Besides, that's the day Sara is supposed to come, and I do not want to have to face that woman. I'm not ready to think about any long term commitment, and she's got marrying on her mind. I'll just volunteer for KP on that day to play it safe."

Sergeant Robbins considered the boy's KP volunteering action as a genuine act of helping his fellow man, and commended him for it. He never saw through Rock's little facade as he arranged the KP duty. On graduation day, the redhead felt quite protected in his little self-manufactured haven. Sara came and Sara went, making him feel even safer.

After the rest of his Company had left for their overseas assignment, Rock made a sweep through each barracks in the entire company area and gathered up every coat hanger he could find. He had in mind a business plan that would make him the next coat-hanger supply king when new recruits checked into those barracks to begin their training. He had seen this business model played out at his expense when he had to purchase his coat hangers on his arrival at Camp Blanding. The new trainees would happily fork over ten cents for each hanger, and Rock could foresee having an extra thirty dollars or more to mail back home to his brother, James, who had set up a savings account for the boy exclusively for his future medical education.

During his extended stay at Camp Blanding, the cadre called on the redhead to help with the intense preparation for the new recruits in the incoming training company. They placed much of the everyday operation of the company, usually handled by non-commissioned officers, in his hands. This led to some experiences that were both interesting and amusing.

With most of his companions for the past 13 weeks of basic training already shipped out, Rock expected the company area would be quite lonely, inactive and boring. The Army and his snafu, crafty, fellow training company washout, Pvt. Roccibola, had quite different ideas.

Someone had told the boy that Roccibola had flunked out of 22 different basic training companies before he joined Company B.

Rumor had it that the soldier had even been in the Army before, and had received a Section Eight discharge after his classification as a psycho. That rumor claimed he had changed his name to Roccibola and joined the Army again. When he was assigned to Company B, Captain Coffman made a special project of seeing that this chronic snafu would finally finish with the rest of Company B, and he gave the guy far more personal attention than any other soldier in his command. However, Roccibola knew far too many tricks. He beat Captain Coffman at every turn. Because the captain did not know all the nuances of the game, Roccibola had flunked-out of the training again and was waiting to be reassigned to his 24th training unit.

Except for the cadre of B Company who were awaiting their new trainees, Pvt. Roccibola, Pvt. Cowart, who was recently discharged from the hospital after treatment for pneumonia, and Rock were the only troops left in the company area. The cadre, of course, wanted as much time off as possible between training companies, so they assigned the redhead as Charge of Quarters (CQ). The very first night the boy sat in the CQ office, Pvt. Cowart came rushing excitedly into the office almost screaming, "Come quickly, Roccibola is about to kill himself."

With all of the staff off post, the redhead knew of no one to call. None of the Army field manuals he had ever read covered a situation such as this, and even Sergeant Rathiewicz from his high school ROTC had not prepared him for this emergency. He had to handle this one on his own, and he did not know what to do.

He dug deeply into his think tank and remembered a tale someone had told him in a Psychology class. This person had claimed the proper thing to do with a male person threatening to take his life was to belittle him, and to curse him as you approached to try to stop him from killing himself. Thinking of using cursing in a positive way made this one of the few times in his life when the boy had any spark of appreciation for his old nemesis, Blackie, the mule. She had armed his vocabulary with enough curse words to use for any occasion.

That late at night, the barracks were dark, so Rock entered the building by the door adjacent to the light switch. When he turned on the lights, he could see Roccibola standing half-crouched over the rifle rack at the opposite end of the 120 foot-long barracks. Thankfully, the rifle rack remained properly locked, so the officers in charge could not hold him responsible for the problem. However, Roccibola had put a 30-30 cartridge into the chamber of one of the rifles in the rack and had his finger on its trigger with his chin resting over the muzzle end of the loaded weapon.

Trying not to let his own insecurity show, Rock launched into a tirade of curse words and epithets that would have made even Sgt. Robbins proud. "Roccibola," he said, "You are about as low as any @^*%@ creature God ever made, if God really did make you. Go ahead, pull the @*^%@ trigger. I don't believe you have the @*^%@ guts to do it." The boy continued to yell his slurs and obscenities as he advanced towards his quarry.

"It's a shame to waste the Army's good ammunition just to get rid of a no good @^*%@ creature like you—and it's an even greater shame for us to be forced to make some worthwhile GI clean up the bloody mess where your blood and brains, if you've got any brains at all, have spilled all over our floor. The least you can do is let me put a *@%^* mattress cover down to protect the floor before you pull that @^*%@ trigger," he continued with the harangue as he inched ever closer to the potential suicide victim.

When Rock reached a point about twenty feet from where his quarry stood, Roccibola suddenly pulled back the bolt of the rifle to eject the bullet. He picked up the rifle cartridge from the floor and flung it through the open door and across the company area. "You won't stop me next time." he whimpered to Rock as he lay down in his bed. "I'll slash both of my wrists and I might even cut my jugular vein."

"Just be sure you notify me before you do anything like that so I can put some extra mattress covers on your bed to absorb the@^*%@ blood," said Rock as he left for the CQ office. "It would be a %#*(% shame for the Army to lose a good mattress because of the @^*%@ likes of you."

The boy did not dare let anyone see him tremble and shed a few tears in the security of the CQ office after that experience.

When the new recruits came on base, the cadre gave the boy considerable responsibility in their orientation. This gave him plenty of exposure to carry out his coat hanger business plan. Thirty dollars amounted to a whole lot more than a full month's pay for an army private in 1945, and the boy happily added it to the $20.00 he already saved from that $21.00 monthly stipend. It was the easiest money he had ever made, and the new troops were happy to have the coat hangers. Both sides were winners.

Transfer to Fort Benning for OCS suited Rock wonderfully well. From there, he could catch a bus and spend an occasional weekend at home with his family. The boy especially liked the stop at Lagrange where girls from Lagrange College sometimes boarded the bus, although that never amounted to anything more than eye-candy for him.

About midway of his training in OCS, the surrender of the Germans to the Allied forces brought great elation to the boy and to most of the world. Nevertheless, Rock's projected assignment remained as Captain Hoffman had outlined it, to help gain the surrender of the Japanese, so he must continue to press forward.

He had expected the academic and physical curriculum in OCS to be exceedingly demanding. As it panned out, the only stress he suffered came as he struggled to make the required minimum number of pull-ups for his physical agility test. That always proved to be very difficult for him because his thighs and rump were large and muscular, and he had never learned a technique to employ them to assist in the exercise. Even though he had done the same exercises in his PT class with the Navy at Mercer, he had to be happy with the minimum number of pull-ups and move on.

He was amazed that Sergeant Rathiewicz had already covered in high school ROTC everything he heard in the OCS classroom, so the mental part seemed second nature. When he received his commission as a Second Lieutenant in the US Army Reserve, he breathed a silent tribute to his old high school mentor. When his gold bars were pinned on him by his mother, the boy could not help but think, *it's funny that I'm not physically fit to study medicine in the Navy, and here they are getting me ready to lead a platoon of soldiers in combat in the Army.*

After his OCS graduation, Rock reported to Camp Joseph T. Robinson near Little Rock, Arkansas where he served as a training officer for recruits preparing for the invasion of Japan. Being responsible for the well being and training of his own platoon meant a lot to the redhead and he took it seriously. Who knew but what someday when they went overseas, his own life could hinge on how well he trained these soldiers for combat. He had to see that they were thoroughly and well trained.

At Camp Robinson, he also learned the hard fact that even though an officer's salary is higher than that of an enlisted man, his expenses were also much higher. His monthly savings for medical school became erratic at best, and most months it was considerably less than when the Army supplied everything for him—but Captain Coffman had said it was his solemn duty to become an officer, and he would do his duty.

The training of Rock's platoon had been about two-thirds completed when word came of two atomic bombs dropped on Japan, and of the unconditional surrender of that nation. It seemed hard for his recruits to show as much interest in training now that the enemy had thrown in the towel, but the training had to be completed. With that accomplished, his orders came to report to a course of instruction at Fort Lee, Virginia, to attend what most of its students called "The Ghoul School."

At first, Rock did not like the fact that the Infantry had loaned him to the Quartermaster Corps, and it impressed him even less to find that his job would be in the graves registration division. For the next two weeks, as he studied how to survey areas to locate American service members buried in the countryside of Europe, he came to the realization that these men deserved the honor and dignity of a proper burial. They had given their lives for their country and the boy would have the privilege of seeing them have a decent burial where the family wished, at home or in the US Military Cemeteries in Europe. He decided it was not a bad deal after all, and it should prepare him for anything gruesome he would face in medical School.

From Fort Lee, the redhead received orders to report to Fort Hamilton, New York to wait for debarkation orders to France and his assignment to a Graves Registration group forming there. With almost no money to spend and too much time on his hands, he found New York quite boring, so he and some buddies used the subways for entertainment. On one of the subway rides, he spotted a good-looking girl with reddish hair and told his friend, McCorkle, "I'm going to take that girl home tonight."

McCorkle said, "You'll never do it. I double-dog-dare you."

Rock, who had never had an official date in his life, said, "I'll take that dare," and he set to work.

He soon learned that her name was Honey and she was not married; she lived in an apartment near Fort Hamilton, and she definitely did not need anyone to walk her home that night. It took a few minutes to overcome her resistance, but Rock soon waved good-bye to McCorkle as the two redheads left the subway hand in hand.

When they reached the door to her apartment complex, Honey said, "You said you were going to walk me home. Well, this is my home. Goodnight."

"Oh no," protested Rock, "this is just the door to your complex. Your home is inside."

"Okay. Come on in. I guess it won't do any harm," said Honey as she brought out her key and opened the door to usher him in.

The next thing Rock knew, Honey nestled cozily in his arms and his lips met hers as he had close physical contact with a girl for the first time in his life. He was the one who had to back away when she suggested going to bed together. The boy found he did not have as smooth a line for turning off the heat as he had for turning it on. Finally, he stammered, "I've never done anything like that before and I had not planned on its going that far tonight."

He left Honey's apartment late that night carrying with him her address and her joshing admonition to "write me and let me know about the lucky girl who first gets you to succumb."

The following day, along with thousands of other troops, he boarded the Queen Mary for his maiden ocean voyage. He felt doubly fortunate to have a room on a level that was not below deck and not to be responsible for any troops on the trip. The latter condition did not last long. A Company of black Quartermaster troops was traveling with only their First Sergeant, and Lt. Notleks received a temporary assignment as their on-board commander. The redhead did not know anything about the duties of these soldiers, and he quickly told First Sergeant Smith, "Just carry on as usual."

At the first assembly of his assigned Company, Rock could not help but be amused as Sergeant Smith used a long string of the strongest expletives before he said to his troops, "Men, there are some WAC's (Women's Army Corps) on this boat and I want you to show some respect for them. I don't want to hear no %*@,%^<% cussin' from any of you @^*%@ guys."

After seeing solid evidence that Sgt. Smith had the company under complete control, the boy relaxed and decided to enjoy the rest of the trip. On his arrival at the dreary, rainy port area of Antwerp, Belgium, he welcomed the arrival of transportation to take him to board a bus for an overland trip to Paris. He had studied French for two quarters at Mercer and had made an "A" in each course. He felt certain he would do well with the language in France.

The next day when he wanted directions to the Louvre, he brought out his best Southern French pronunciation and asked a passerby in his slow Southern drawl, "Pardonnez moi, mai ou est La Louvre?" Her answer came in such rapid and undecipherable banter that the boy simply turned around and went back to his quarters. He never again tried to find the museum. However, he had absolutely no problem understanding the girls that grasped his hand or arm as he walked down the street and begged, "Aw, come on, Joe." Nor did his refusal of each offer of personal services seem to be difficult. The Army's educational program had been quite effective with this redhead in that area—and then, there was his religious conviction.

Even Les Folies Begere could not hold the boy's full attention because he could not understand one word the actors were saying. Greatly disappointed at his total failure in the arena of language, he boarded the bus for the over road trip to Marseilles, France, where his new outfit, the 385th Quartermaster Group, awaited.

A GROUP OF ROCKHEADS

The 385th Quartermaster Group was temporarily located in Aix-en-Provence, France. Newly formed for the purpose of grave registration, it writhed in its early coming-into-existence throes when an acne-pocked "shave-tail" named Rock arrived to join its ranks. The boy had compiled quite a bit of scoop on his new organization as he reported for duty. He knew that the group was a part of the 12th American Grave Registration Command (AGRC), designed to be a semi-mobile, somewhat nomadic force with assigned areas of responsibility beginning in France, then on to Germany and Austria. The group planned to dispatch small units into tiny hamlets as well as large cities as they scoured their previously mapped territory in search of bodies of American service members buried by local citizens in locations other than American military cemeteries.

From what Rock could hear about its composition, the fledgling outfit appeared to be doomed to disastrous failure because of its makeup. Half of its officers, himself included, came directly from the States with no previous command experience. Most of them were very young and inexperienced "90-day wonders" (graduates of officer candidate schools). These young officers had become surplus commodity now that the atomic blasts at Hiroshima and

Nagasaki had brought the war with Japan to a sudden halt. They had not drawn the assignment for this sordid duty because of their outstanding preparation and qualifications. The Army simply assigned them here because they were surplus, and neither the Graves Registration Command nor its officers were important in the overall post war scheme. Rock was typical of this group.

The other half of its officers came mostly as castoffs from combat organizations. Now that the war was over and their most important tasks were completed, these outfits were trimming down to save money. Scuttlebutt among the troops said requests for these troops came only as a generic call for a specific number of officers of each specified rank (i.e. so many captains, majors, colonels, etc.) No commanding officer in his right mind—even of a unit that was trimming down—would ship out his top leadership in response to a generic call. He would send his deadheads and goof-offs—and that is what they did.

That generalization certainly appeared to hold true among the new officers of the 385th who came from those downsizing outfits. In most cases, the organization that shipped an officer to the newly formed group must have felt they improved their own capabilities by getting rid of an incompetent.

Exactly the same problems were associated with the selection of enlisted men. One-third of these men came as green recruits directly from a basic training routine that had prepared them, not for graves registration, but for the now unnecessary invasion of Japan. By definition, raw recruits had no experience.

A second third of the enlisted personnel for the fledgling organization, including most of the non commissioned officers, also came from the trim down of other outfits after the time of combat had ended. This meant the men who normally are the backbone of any military team received their assignments more because of their lack of ability and conformity than for the possession of the needed skills to do a demanding job. Sad to say, it appeared that a majority of the non commissioned officers in the group were of the same dysfunctional and discarded ilk as were the commissioned officers.

Believe it or not, the final third of enlisted men actually came directly from disbanded detention camps as the Army reduced its troop numbers on the continent. They gave outright pardons to many stockade inmates who had committed what might be termed as lesser offenses or offenses associated with extenuating circumstances. In other words, about one-third of the enlisted men for the 385th came directly from the calaboose.

Most of those with any real experience, both among officers and enlisted personnel, had some form of shell shock or battle fatigue. This combination of factors caused both morale and morals among the troops to be quite low from the get-go, and was the basis for a very interesting, if not for a smoothly functioning, organization. Perhaps that was fitting for an organization like Rock's new assignment. You had to be at least a little kooky to do the work planned for the 385th.

Despite the fact that he had many qualms about his organization, Rock felt happy to participate in the assigned duty of the 385th and search for American service members who had been killed in places where their own outfits could not reclaim their bodies for proper burial. He had learned that most of these heroes were airmen killed on bombing raids but the list also included many soldiers killed in parachuting attacks or covert action behind enemy lines. "*These guys deserve the best I can give them,*" he said to himself.

After locating their gravesites, the Grave Registration units would dig up these heroic men and identify their bodies. Their families could then choose for the remains of their loved ones to be buried in American cemeteries in Europe or be returned home for burial in the USA.

The units would find most of the soldiers' graves poorly marked, as would be expected of burial sites behind enemy lines. In addition, after two or three years, information about these resting places and about their occupants would be sketchy at best. Almost every case would have its own set of individual circumstances, and a different hero rested in the gravesite that marked the end of each trail of evidence that the 385th followed. Rock would soon come to wish that both he and his outfit were better prepared to do proper homage for those who had given their lives for their country in this heroic way and, sometimes, in God-forsaken places.

Occasionally, there would also be a "false-find." These apparent cowards had dug a hole, marked it with their own dog tag nailed to a wooden marker and shagged off to Paris or some other place where they thought life would be more exotic than would ever be possible on a battlefield.

All of this info sloshed in the head of the green, 19-year-old, second lieutenant when he reached his new assignment. It was a Sunday morning when he saluted First Lieutenant Nuzzy, who was in temporary command of the 385th pending the arrival of its permanent commander.

"Hello," grinned the fuzzy-cheeked newcomer, "I'm Lieutenant Notleks. My friends usually call me 'Rock.' I'm newly assigned to the 385th, and am reporting for duty as ordered." Rock chose never to use the demeaning "Second" before his rank of "Lieutenant." He assumed his gold bars, instead of the silver ones denoting a "First Lieutenant," would have already made that point clear.

Nuzzy was of medium build with excessively long, crew cut, brown hair that appeared to be wilting and in sad need of a trim. There was no military bearing about this veteran soldier. He was slightly stoop-shouldered and had permanently unsettled, green eyes that darted defensively right and left without ever fixing on any special object or person. He had a much-greater-than-expected number of wrinkles in his face, giving him the appearance of being much older than his actual age of 32.

A coarse tremor exhibited itself in each of his hands. The tremor showed a marked increase as he sloppily returned Rock's sharp military salute. Rock would hear later of Nuzzy's heroics in the Battle of the Bulge, but he would not hear it from this hero. In earlier times of intense combat, Nuzzy had paid a great price to save the lives of others in his platoon. Yet he never sought any glory for his action, and certainly never took any opportunity to talk about it.

Nuzzy could hardly wait until a permanent commander of the 385th came on board because that would open the door for his release from military service. His time was nearly completed, and he was simply going through the motions of halfway doing his duty until he could get home. Rock had seen enough heroes in his day to recognize this one and to take no offense at Lt. Nuzzy's lack of protocol and his inefficiency.

"Oh, don't give me any of that bull-crap," retorted the irritated temporary commander as he turned aside. "Now where the hell is that mess-sergeant? He's supposed to have my supply of liquor for this week here before this time. He knows I can't operate without that stuff."

Turning back to Rock, he said, "Now, Lieutenant Hot-licks or Hot-lips, or whatever the hell your name is, you've been through the same orientation they put me through when I came into this damned outfit. If you have any sense at all, you know just as much as I do about it. You can find out from the first sergeant what you're supposed to do here. Just do it and don't bother me. I've got some serious drinking to do if that mess-sergeant ever gets herewith my supplies. Get out from here and see the first sergeant. He'll tell you where to bunk. Just get out and don't bother me…

"…Now where the hell is my liquor? Sarge had better hurry with it before I really get the shakes," mumbled the Lieutenant as Rock left the room.

The first sergeant showed Rock a list of jobs that had not been filled in the unit. To his surprise, the job of special investigations officer for the group remained on the list. He had never done anything similar to that before—but, after all, he was just as well qualified to be an investigator as anybody else he had met in this crazy outfit, and he had thought of himself as a detective when he studied math.

If they didn't want me to take it, they should not have left that job on the list when they showed it to me, Rock thought as he filled out the forms indicating his choice was to be the Special Investigations Officer. *Perhaps it won't be as boring as everything else I've done in this man's army before now. I might even find a little adventure.*

Obviously, Lt. Nuzzy did have some serious drinking to do. He stayed day and night in a small, dark room next to the mess-hall, apparently trying to drown the memories of his experiences during "the Bulge," He had frequent short visits from his mess-sergeant friend, Sergeant Blackmon, who looked after his commanding officer and brought him food, liquor and other supplies. Blackmon was one of the soldiers Nuzzy had rescued from a German machine-gun in a bunker on top of a high hill during "the Bulge." The machine gun had pinned his platoon down for three full days with its withering fire, and had picked off several of his platoon members one-by-one.

Only a handful of Sergeant Blackmon's platoon members remained alive when Lt. Nuzzy took matters into his own hand. He took no thought for his own life as he climbed the hill under constant machine-gun fire and tossed in a hand-grenade to wipe out the bunker. Blackmon felt he owed his life to the Lieutenant and took every opportunity to repay this debt. No one dared make any derogatory remarks about Nuzzy's excessive drinking or his inability to cope with his job when Sergeant Blackmon was around.

About two weeks after Rock's arrival, Col. Kilts arrived and Lt. Nuzzy was relieved of his command. The Army transferred him to a military hospital for treatment of acute and chronic alcoholism, prior to his medical discharge from the service.

Sergeant Blackmon was more distraught than he had ever been. Now, who would look after his friend to whom he owed his very life?

LTC. K. I. KILTS, CHIEF ROCKHEAD

THE NEW AND PERMANENT commander of the 385th made his dramatic, quite revealing, though somewhat comic, entrance a day or two before the departure of Lt. Nuzzy. Lieutenant Colonel Kermot Independence Kilts had graduated with top honors from West Point many years prior to this assignment and, according to the Army grapevine, had a reputation for extreme brilliance in his earlier years. In those better times, rumor said he had written an Army field manual that all branches of the military used as a guideline for bivouac of forces in the field. The all-knowing grapevine also claimed that after having made this superb accomplishment, he suffered a serious head injury in a motorcycle accident. That injury exacted a heavy toll on his mental capacity but, after a lengthy period of convalescence, it left him physically capable of continuing his Army service. When he returned to active duty, the Colonel apparently received promotions based solely on his length-of-service and not based on the merit of his performance.

Automatic promotions usually came only up to the rank of Lieutenant Colonel, and Colonel Kilts had wallowed in that rank for the past several years. This aroused some speculation as to what would be his abilities as a commanding officer, and the general consensus among the officers of the unit would soon come to be that Colonel Kilts transfer to the 385th had considerably improved his previous outfit.

Kilts, a six-footer of medium-to-large frame, looked everyday of his claimed age of 51 years. He had a slightly pale complexion with receding light brown hair and unsteady green eyes. His small, wire-framed glasses that slipped down his nose whenever he talked gave him the appearance of looking down his nose at everyone, and most people felt it represented his true personality. He considered himself a great organizer and communicator, and was quite proud of his accomplishments in the military. In his ordinary conversation, the Colonel often repeated his statements or questions, giving an echo effect that he hoped would be dramatic. Only a few short hours after his arrival at group headquarters, the new Group Commander entered the clerical room and asked the hunt-and-peck clerk-typist who was struggling with some forms in his ancient typewriter, "What are you doing? What are you doing?"

"Sir," said the corporal as he jumped to his feet and snapped a salute, "I'm typing a requisition for supplies. We need so many things so badly and we hardly have anything yet. Eventually, we're supposed to have 50 clerk-typists in this outfit, but I'm the only one who has reported for duty so far. Believe it or not, this antique typewriter I'm using is the only typewriter we have. You can look at it and tell it has seen better days."

"Take it out—take it out," demanded the new CO as he swept his outstretched right arm from left to right in dramatic flair and pointed to the form in the ancient typewriter. "I'm about to go on the most important mission of my Army career. Take a letter in six copies."

As soon as the clerk had his pen ready, the Colonel began his monotonous dictation. His words gave every observer quite a shock as the Colonel began "Dear Mable." 'The most important mission' of Kilts army career was a letter to his wife.

Corporal Wilson could not take shorthand, but the harried clerk-typist dutifully took down each word in longhand as rapidly as he could write. Then, he slowly pecked the document out on his dilapidated typewriter, striking the keys hard enough to make five carbon copies. As soon as he had completed his part in this debacle, he handed his new commanding officer all six copies of the letter.

"Here is your letter, sir," said Corporal Wilson, saluting sharply. He tried hard to repress the grin that nearly broke out across his face despite his efforts.

"What? What? Oh, yes," said the daydreaming Kilts as he took the six-copy document. "Thank you, Corporal. It looks as if you did a good job."

Holding six copies of the letter in his hand, the new commanding officer reached into his desk drawer and pulled out six envelopes. He marked "free" in the space for postage, and addressed all six of the envelopes to his wife. He then inserted one copy of the letter into each envelope and licked the glued surface of the first envelope to seal it lightly. He inserted the lightly sealed letter into the middle of his huge desktop dictionary, which he promptly placed on the floor. The Colonel insured he had sealed each letter well by jumping up and down on the dictionary while singing in an undistinguished, loud voice, *The Last Time I Saw Paris*.

Col. Kilts proceeded to seal all six copies of the letter in the exact same manner. He then handed the finished products to Corporal Wilson for mailing—all to the same address and to his wife. Officers and enlisted men of the 385th watched the bizarre scene in shock and amazement at this first of many pieces of evidence that their new commander had fallen victim to a severe posttraumatic psychosis, with his major fixation being on mail. At the same time, they reported almost to a man, a sense of sympathy for the Colonel's poor wife.

Colonel Kilts demonstrated his deep, pathological mail fixation in many different ways and on several different occasions. One example of that malady often occurred as he read a magazine, typically printed four or five years earlier. He would dramatically tear out a page, fold it and put it into an envelope. He would then address the envelope to his wife and mail it without any comment or explanation. Rock could not help but wonder if the poor woman worried herself silly about this quirk in his behaviour or was she glad she did not have to put up with him at home. He would definitely have voted for the latter.

In spite of the fact that their top-level leadership appeared grossly incapable of doing its job, the time came when the personnel roster for the 385th was complete and the group received orders to move to its assigned location in the city of Lyon in Central France. This proved to be quite a hectic time for Colonel Kilts, as the move obviously presented great tactical problems for him. As he fumed and fussed over even the most minor detail of this transfer, the Colonel often put his thoughts into words clearly heard by those around him.

"God, if I only had a stenographer," said the Colonel, using for the first time in Rock's presence an interjected phrase the redhead would hear many times during the coming months. "She could put down these important thoughts for me, and I could move on to other things.

"I have so many things to do, there is no possible way I can finish them all before we have to leave. I've got to write to my wife, my son, my daughter, my sister and my brother…and then there are all of the details of this move to Lyon…" His muttered thoughts trailed off. Rock considered this statement quite strange because he knew that the first four persons on the colonel's verbal list were residents of the same house. It seemed logical to the redhead that he could communicate with all of those at one address with one letter.

Suddenly the commander snapped his fingers and, apparently impressed with his own brilliance, jubilantly turned to Corporal Wilson. "Corporal," he said, "I know what I'll do. Take a letter in six copies. 'Dear blank,'" the colonel dictated and then turned back to Corporal Wilson.

"Now, Corporal," he said, "you just leave the spot for the name blank and I'll fill it in later when I sign the letters," he explained before he began to dictate again.

Corporal Wilson laboriously cranked out the dictated letter with, as per his instructions, a blank space for the addressee's name.

When he had completed his task, he handed all six copies of the letter to Colonel Kilts. "Here are your letters, Sir," the corporal said—but by now, he had abandoned the salute of respect.

"What? What?...Oh, yes, yes, the letters to my family. Thank you Corporal. Remind me that I want to promote you to sergeant, you are doing such a good job," said Kilts as he took the letters and turned back to his desk.

"Now let me see...God, if I only had a stenographer, she could put down my important thoughts," mused Kilts aloud as he began to separate copies of the letter. "I have six copies here. I will mail the original to my wife, this copy to my son, this one to my daughter, this to my sister and that one to my brother," as he laid the copies across his desk. "Hmmm...now let me see...that's one, two, three, four, five copies...but I have six copies of the letter."

Scratching his head as if in deep thought, he said aloud, "I'm too busy and too important a man to waste the time I put into writing that copy of the letter...What should I do with it? Now let me see... Oh, yes... Sergeant Wilson, come here."

Corporal—or was he really Sergeant—Wilson saluted this time as he stood at attention before Colonel Kilts and crisply said, "Yes, Sir."

"Wilson," Colonel Kilts began his dissertation with obvious self-satisfaction, "you already have the information as to what our mailing address will be when we move to Lyon. You take charge of this copy of this letter for me so we will not waste it. You know that waste in the Army is one of my pet peeves."

"Yes, Sir," snapped Wilson in reply, "and what would the Colonel have me to do with his letter?"

Kilts replied as he left the room, "I will be going to Lyon in the morning. Just mail it to me in Lyon."

In this manner, the intrepid 385th Quartermaster Battalion prepared for transfer to its first field area in Graves Registration based out of Lyon, France. Rock moved closer to the uncharted waters of his work as a special investigations officer. Both he and his new unit were equally unprepared for their tasks.

The arrangements made by Colonel Kilts for housing of the 385th were as strange as the Colonel himself. In his plan, housing for all of the enlisted personnel was in an old abandoned French Army camp located in a relatively inaccessible area 12 miles from town. The camp was extremely antiquated and, according to US standards, the French had planned it poorly in the beginning. The soldiers stationed there thought the French would have abandoned it even if the Germans had not so quickly conquered their country.

The barracks were woefully rundown structures replete with inadequate showers and faulty, foul-smelling latrine facilities. A soldier in the shower stood in danger of being either scalded or frozen when another turned on the water or flushed a toilet. The one reasonably nice building in the entire camp area was taken over and refurbished by the non-commissioned officers to serve as the NCO club.

For an enlisted man, transportation into Lyon was a knotty problem indeed. A soldier on pass had to walk a couple of miles from camp to reach the end of the streetcar-line, unless he happened to catch a ride from the camp. He could then board a streetcar and ride into town for a few francs.

Colonel Kilts repeatedly denied the enlisted men's requests for a shuttle bus from camp into town or, at least, to the end of the public transportation line. He declared it was too expensive and could not be justified at a time when the Army was scaling back its forces. To add to the problem, even the streetcars ceased operation at midnight, so there could be no late nights on the town for the enlisted men of the 385th.

On the other hand, the officers' billets were in the old Grand Hotel near the center of town, with a beautiful view overlooking the placid flow of the Rhone River. The hotel had been a truly magnificent structure in its day, but the ravages of time and of war had taken their toll on both its beauty and function.

The stark contrast between the quarters assigned to the enlisted personnel and those for its officers became an understandable constant source of irritation to the soldiers. Add to that the ghoulish nature of the work they were learning to perform and an almost total absence of good leadership at the higher echelons, morale of the troops soon sunk to abysmal lows.

Rock could hardly believe his own good fortune in his room assignment. It far surpassed all of the other places where he had lived before, either in or out of the Army. His assigned room was a very large one on a corner of the second floor of the hotel overlooking a beautiful park along the river's edge. For the first time in his life, he had his very own bathroom. It did not matter that the fixtures were antique and functioned poorly. It certainly far outdistanced the old outhouse he had grown up having to depend on for those needed functions.

There was, however, one strange looking fixture inside his room. It stood just outside the bathroom door, and totally baffled the boy as to what purpose it might serve. It looked somewhat like a china drinking fountain, but it had both hot and cold water running to it—and who would want to drink hot water?

When you turned the handle for either cold or hot water, a stream of water spurted up and fell back into the bowl just like the water fountains he had seen when he was in Paris. However, this fixture stood just short of knee high—almost on the floor. You would have to get on your knees to get a drink of water here. Even a country bumpkin like Rock knew there was something incomplete about his understanding of the thing, but he was too proud to ask anyone what the fixture might be.

One day as Lieutenant Wilcox visited his room, Rock finally summoned up the nerve to ask, "Dan, what in the world is that contraption?"

Wilcox responded with a laugh, "Oh, that's right. You're one of those dumb old-timey country Baptists from Georgia where your plumbing is outdoors. You would never in this world know what a thing such as a bidet is."

"A what kind of day?" replied Rock with a quizzical look on his face.

"I said a bidet, spelled b-i-d-e-t" continued Dan, now in almost hysterical laughter. "You know, it's a woman kind of thing. She squats down right over it and squirts clean, warm water on her private parts to make herself clean. It sure beats that old red rubber douche bag with the long rubber hose and nozzle most of our women in America still use…or do yawl use those corncobs in Georgia for that, too?"

Dan was still laughing as he left the room.

Rock made absolutely certain the door to his room was locked tightly when he pretended to be a girl using this contraption. As he turned on the water nice and warm, a small light of understanding about the function of that fixture began to dawn.

Colonel Kilts had made no provision for office space within the hotel for the several different units that made up the 385th, yet he insisted that there be a room specified as headquarters for each of the paper organizations that made up his command. Rock thought the idea was foolish for such a small unit. However, the Colonel directed that his own room would serve as Battalion headquarters and Rock's room would function nicely as Company headquarters. He designated other officer's rooms to be headquarters for the smaller units that filled out the organizational chart of the 385th.

One day as Rock was walking down the hallway from his room (Company headquarters), Colonel Kilts emerged from the shower and headed toward his room (Battalion headquarters). With the exception of an oversized towel shrouded about his waist, he was naked.

"Lieutenant Notleks, I want to see you in Battalion Headquarters right away," the Colonel called on seeing his subordinate officer.

Rock quickly readjusted his course and went to the Colonel's room. He was shocked and embarrassed to see his commanding officer lying completely naked on his bed.

"You wanted to see me, Sir?" Rock questioned as he rendered the required salute.

"What? What? Oh, yes," said Kilts. "Now let me see…what was it I wanted to speak to you about…God, if I only had a stenographer, she could put down these important thoughts…Now let me think…"

Rock tried hard to keep his composure and not show his true emotions as the mental picture of a stenographer recording the Colonel's thoughts in this particular situation flitted through his mind. He feigned a cough to hide his smile and to quell his almost irresistible urge to laugh.

After what seemed an inordinately long period when Rock had to gaze on the naked body of his superior officer, Kilts finally snapped his fingers and said with a great sense of excitement. "I knew it had to be something very important for me to call you into headquarters…

"Lieutenant Notleks, the morale among our troops is terrible. We have to do something. We have to do something and we have to get it done right away, or we just might have a mutiny on our hands. These men have got to have Ping-Pong balls."

It is certainly much better to quell a mutiny with Ping-Pong balls than to have to put it down with rifle balls the way Snuffy Smith does in the funny papers, Rock thought as he shuffled off to the supply clerk to place a hurry up order for the unit's needed recreational equipment.

Col. Kilts continued his self-acclaimed "brilliant" management of the 385th, requiring officers meetings at 10 a.m. and at 2:00 p.m. daily. Regardless of his efforts, the organization fell further and further behind in its assigned work of scouring the countryside around Lyon for graves of their fallen comrades. To the redhead, it seemed an impossibility to make progress and still attend two officer's meetings every day…especially when so much red tape and acrimony were a part of those meetings.

Several weeks passed with very little progress in the assigned tasks of the unit. One day, Major Robert Thornton, who Rock thought was the unit's most capable officer when he was "on the wagon," presented the morning officer's meeting with an idea that promised to bring some progress.

"We cover an assigned area with a radius of slightly over 200 kilometers surrounding Lyon. That is just too far for us to send out our field units on a daily basis. We spend too much time in travel, and our teams are tired by the time they arrive at the sites. Then they have too little time for their work assignments.

"Lieutenant Thomas has done an excellent job of getting his platoon organized for the work we need to do. I think he is ready now for us to send him and his unit out of Lyon and into a surrounding area to do some of our work. We know that they will have to move their base of operation every few weeks as they clear an area, but Lieutenant Thomas and I have discussed that, and I am certain he knows how to secure housing and he can handle the work."

The officers in the unit thoroughly discussed and finally approved Major Thornton's plan. At last, the 385th would begin its work in earnest, even though it was only at about one-fourth of its expected capacity. News of their early activity in the area around Lyon apparently spread rapidly in the civilian community, and reports of American service members buried in more rural areas around the city began to come in rapid-fire order.

Lt. Thomas' platoon had been in the field for only a few days when Col. Kilts called Rock into Battalion headquarters. "Lieutenant Notleks," he began, "I want you to meet Pierre Gusteau. He has told me a story that I feel should be checked into by our special investigations officer."

Rock's heart seemed to jump completely into his throat at the simple thought he was going to have to do an actual investigation.

"Monsieur Gusteau," Kilts continued, "this is Lieutenant Notleks, our special investigations officer. You can tell him your story."

Pierre began a story of great intrigue that made Rock truly eager to begin his work so he could find out more. The story suddenly became a matter of personal curiosity, and he felt he had to pursue it to its conclusion even if only to satisfy his own curiosity. The redhead now had to truly become an investigator.

The young Frenchman began, "My brother, Robert, God rest his soul, was a member of the...how do you say...French Resistance movement during the latter parts of the war. He caused those hated Nazis a lot of trouble, and he was very smart about it. For a long time the Germans did not even suspect him, but he was finally trapped and arrested by those...how do you say...bastards, just a few weeks before the American soldiers came into France.

"With the help of the French underground, Robert was able to smuggle a letter out of the prison to me. His letter gave me a few details of what was happening in the prison and a list of the men who were captives there. We were trying to plan a way for their escape, but just before those Nazis bastards retreated, they lined up 52 of those patriots and shot them in cold blood. They did not even bother to bury them. They left them lying on the ground exactly where they fell," continued Gusteau as he brushed back a tear.

"My brother, Robert, was in that group of heroes. And there was also a young man named Edmond Bonnard. Robert told me that this fellow, Bonnard, was an American citizen of some sort, but I cannot be certain whether he was a soldier or on some secret mission. Really, Monsieur Lieutenant, I had met Bonnard before those beastly cowards arrested him and I could not detect one trace of American accent in his speech. From my talking to him, I am not certain that he was an American."

Rock had been listening breathlessly and with his heart pounding rapidly up until this point, but now felt it his duty to assume his role as investigator. "Could it be possible that he might have been a serviceman smuggled in by the army to help your brother's unit or even a member of the CIA or some other undercover agency sent here to help the French Resistance?" Rock suggested.

"That is what I believe, Monsieur," replied Pierre as he pulled an envelope from his pocket. "Like I have already say, I do not know if he was even from America but Robert did succeed in sending a picture of some of the men. It is not very clear, but that is my brother, Robert, in the back row and I think this man is Monsieur Edmond Bonnard." He pulled out a photograph and pointed to a short, thin man standing in the front row.

Gusteau handed his prized possession photograph to the redhead. It proved to be a very poorly focused picture of a dozen men. The picture showed evidence of considerable wear from excessive handling. Pierre could not control his sobbing as he parted with his picture.

Each one of the men in the picture appeared quite thin and haggard and they showed, without exception, considerable evidence of poor treatment. Despite their stated youth, they all looked like old men.

"Robert was only 24," Gusteau whispered as he brushed away a tear from his cheek.

"He was certainly a fine looking young man," Rock asserted, ignoring the evidence to the contrary shown in the photo, "and I am certain you are very, very proud of what he tried to do for your country."

"Oui, Monsieur Lieutenant. Of course, I am very proud of him. I was not there when those bastards shot him, but I am certain that Robert's last words were 'Vive la France.' He wanted all of France to live in freedom and he was willing to die for it," said Pierre before his voice trailed off.

"But back to Edmond Bonnard. He is the real reason I came here to see you. As I have say, I think that is him…right there in the first row of the picture," Pierre continued as he pointed to a blurred image in his precious photo. "Perhaps the police may be able to show you some better pictures in their files at headquarters. They just might even have positive identification, even fingerprints, and more information about him.

"I suppose you already know that the people built a very big monument in memory of the 52 men—right there where they were shot and left on the ground. My Mama and I were there the day the memorial was dedicated."

Colonel Kilts spoke up as soon as Pierre finished speaking, "Lt. Notleks, I want you to find out about this Bonnard fellow. He might not have been one of our service members, but who really knows who he was or from where he came or what he was doing here? You are our Special Investigations Officer, and this surely sounds like a special situation to me. Keep me informed about what you find."

Rock was thrilled and terrified at the same time about his first task as a special investigations officer. *How in this world will I ever go about trying to find one man in 52 with no more to go on than I have now? Man, I sure do wish I had some more training for this job. Oh well*, he mused, *at least it will succeed in getting me out of those boring two-a-day officers meetings for a little while.*

The boy immediately began the heretofore completely unfamiliar task of interviewing the various officials of the small village in the remote suburb of Lyon where the massacre had taken place. His instructors in "The Ghoul School" at Fort Lee had told him that the office of the mayor was usually a proper starting point for investigations into any death. The Chief of Police, Fire Chief and Parish Priest followed in order.

The Mayor was relatively new in his office and had little or no knowledge of the case of Edmond Bonnard. However, he saw the opportunity for political gain here and he wanted to show Rock the beautiful monument the city had built in honor of these brave men who had given their lives for the cause of freedom. Of course, he arranged for the local photographer to be present for what he considered a very important interview with the American Lieutenant.

The Police Chief was out of his office that day but the Fire Chief had a moderate amount of knowledge about the case in general. However, he could not provide Rock with any pictures or facts that were specific enough to give further insight into the identity of Monsieur Bonnard, or the individual identity of any of the deceased.

From the open arms with which the Parish Priest welcomed Rock to his humble parish, one might have surmised the redhead had liberated France single-handedly. The young investigator, still actually a teenager, tried to get down to business immediately. However, he was overwhelmed with the priest's offers of French bonbons, American cigarettes and a glass of his very best French wine. Always a huge chowhound, Rock quickly accepted and devoured the candies, as he engaged in normal small talk with the accommodating priest. The cleric instantly accepted Rock's simple disclaimer of, "Thank you, but I do not smoke." and put away the pack of cigarettes.

However, the same polite "Thank you, but I do not drink," was met with insistence on the part of the cleric. He filled two small crystal wine glasses with an almost perfectly clear liquid the novice Lieutenant assumed to be a very dry white wine. The boy's persistent objections of "I do not drink," fell on deaf Catholic ears as the priest raised his glass and his voice in a toast to America and to the freedom France now enjoyed. He encouraged—in fact, he insisted—that the boy do the same.

As the priest turned up his glass, Rock felt he had no choice but to comply. He, too, turned up his glass of wine and took a swallow. It felt as if his throat was on fire and both of his ears burned. To him, the taste seemed just the same as he imagined the taste of pure varnish would be. Hurriedly, he emptied his glass and began his questioning of the priest. Rock was afraid he might become drunk and pass out on the spot, so he did not prolong the interview. After he concluded the priest had even less information than did the mayor, he was ready to go.

Thank God, thought the naive young officer as he wound up the interview, *I do have a driver. He can take me back to the hotel and I don't have to drive home drunk*. Rock returned to his room and went to bed as quickly as possible.

The next day when the redhead found the Police Chief in his office, he found that this official had really done his homework and done it well. He was able to produce pictures and finger prints of each of the 52 men, identifying the occupant of gravesite #50 as Monsieur Edmond Bonnard. Rock was quite elated to know where Bonnard was, but now began the even more arduous task of finding out who this mysterious possible American citizen could possibly be.

Was Bonnard a spy for the Americans? an agent of the CIA? or was he just a French patriot? Local opinion proved definitely divided on this matter. Some claimed to remember his growing up in the local community, but nobody could remember any other member of his family or the specific location where they had lived. Others claimed to remember distinctly Bonnard's having appeared seemingly from nowhere, not too long after the German occupation of France. Still others said he had come on the scene only a few weeks or months before Robert Gusteau's arrest. Thus, the mystery deepened.

At least, Rock felt certain he had determined that Bonnard was not a regular member of the American armed forces and, therefore, would not be included in his area of responsibility. He assembled every shred of information he had garnered and forwarded it to the FBI headquarters in Washington, DC, requesting instructions as to how he should proceed on the case.

The FBI never returned any instructions or even an acknowledgment of receipt of the information to the redhead. He assumed he had stumbled onto something that might affect the national security, and that in effect, his investigation was over, although nothing would ever satisfy his curiosity. He reluctantly returned to Group Headquarters and those intolerable two-a-day officer's meetings.

One morning shortly after the redhead's return to the 385th, there appeared at the dreaded morning officer's meeting a very distinguished looking, elderly Lieutenant-Colonel escorted by Col. Kilts. He was fairly short in stature, with light blue eyes that squinted noticeably in any light, reminding Rock remarkably of an owl. He had close-cropped white hair and a perfectly trimmed, white mustache that bore a yellow stain from cigarette smoke in its central part. He wore a gorgeous Eisenhower type jacket made from a material that Rock could not recognize. It bothered the redhead greatly that the colonel allowed the ashes from his cigarette to fall on the jacket and remain there until he had completed smoking that cigarette.

However, when he lit a new cigarette from the butt of the previous one, he meticulously cleaned every vestige of ash from the jacket, a ritual that seemed to captivate every eye at that meeting. *The material in that jacket must be a miracle fabric to clean that well*, the redhead thought after the mystery Colonel completed his brushing task.

At precisely 10:00 a.m., (the Colonel was punctual if nothing else), Col. Kilts began the officer's meeting with, "Officers of the 385th, I want to present to you Lieutenant-Colonel Jean Balladay. Col. Balladay has just transferred here and I assume he has orders to take over command of the 385th Quartermaster Battalion."

To Rock's great surprise, every officer of the 385th repressed his cheer—or it could have been that Col. Balladay was too quick to voice his objection, "My orders just tell me to report for duty. They don't say a thing about my taking over command of this unit."

"Well, indeed," exclaimed the completely flustered Kilts. "I suppose I just assumed you outranked me because of your white hair…By the way," he continued, "What is your date-of-rank as a Lieutenant Colonel?"

"January 23, 1940," Colonel Balladay responded immediately, showing a tone of reverence in his voice, "the day my Army Reserve outfit was called to active duty to serve our country. That was a mighty proud day for me."

Col. Kilts was obviously still agitated as he responded, "I'm sure it was a proud day for you, Colonel Balladay, but it looks as if we still have a problem here. That is the same day I received my promotion to the same rank. Tell me, what time of day did your notification of promotion come?"

"Now let me see," Balladay expressed his thoughts aloud, "it seems to me it was about noon...Yes, it was exactly noon of January 23, 1940."

Kilts seemed even more befuddled now as he continued to try to unravel the puzzle of which one outranked the other and should be in command. "That makes things even more confusing, Colonel," he said, "because it's the same exact date and time that I received my notification...Now let me see...What time zone were you in when your promotion came through?"

"My Army Reserve outfit was located in Oklahoma City, Oklahoma, so that would be in the central time zone, wouldn't it?" responded Balladay.

"Yes. Then, I guess that settles it," said Kilts as he blew a sigh of relief. "I was in Fort Belvoir, Virginia, at the time. That is in the eastern time zone, which is an hour ahead of central time. I outrank you by one hour, Colonel. I suppose that means I am still in command."

Every officer of the 385th slumped in defeat at the news that Colonel Kilts had withstood this challenge to his leadership and would continue as their commanding officer. Their disappointment was so keenly felt and so deep; they could hardly even chuckle at the comic scene that had just played out before them.

Here were two high-ranking officers who did not know what almost every junior officer knew: when your dates-of-present rank were exactly the same, the senior officer would always be the one who had the earlier date-of-rank in the previously held grade. The hour these officers received their notification of their promotion to their present rank should have had no bearing at all on who assumed command of the 385th.

Now, the only hope for the 385th was that the Medical Review Board would respond favorably to the evidence submitted by the Group Medical Officer, Captain Schmedley. In his report, he outlined his reasons for his diagnosis of Posttraumatic Psychosis for Colonel Kilts. Dr. Schmedley, too, was convinced that the outfit would never be able to function in a proper manner until it had an officer at its helm that held complete command of most of his faculties.

ROCK-BOTTOM IN COMMANDERS

Dan Wilcox's voice exuded great excitement as he burst into Rock's room completely out of breath. "Rock, have you heard the latest news?" he blustered. "You will not believe what's happened."

"What news are you babbling about this time, Dan?" Rock responded without any evidence of great interest. "It's always something with you, but it must be something really big this time to have you this excited. Have those dad-gum Russians finally attacked us, or what is it?"

"No. No. It's not anything bad," Wilcox continued with jubilation, "but old Kilts is out—gone—kaput, The Medical Review Board adopted the report that Captain Schmedley sent to them and they agree the Colonel has that 'Post-Traumatic Psychosis' stuff, or whatever those big words were that Schmedley used.

"They have already relieved him from active duty and plan to place him in a hospital to get him stabilized before he is medically discharged from the Army. All the guys are down at the bar celebrating. Maybe we'll get someone here who knows something more about what's going on in the world."

Secretly, Rock's heart went out to the old man even though he knew in that same heart that Kilt's departure would be absolutely in the best interest of the 385th. *The colonel has never known any other home as an adult except the Army, and to have had a brilliant career wiped out by a stupid motorcycle accident. It just isn't right*, the redhead mused.

"I hope they've got somebody else in mind to replace Kilts as the commander besides that old fogy, Colonel Balladay," Rock complained aloud. "He's so old; I believe he has to remember when dirt was invented. Man, I don't believe he has had an original idea since he showed enough smarts to stow away on Noah's ark. All he really knows how to do is to smoke those nasty old cigarettes and brush off the ashes after they fall on that beautiful Ike jacket of his. Oh yes, I forgot. He can mumble. He talks like he's got a mouthful of grits all the time."

"Oh, Rock, that's all you Southern boys can ever think about… eating those cruddy old grits," Dan Wilcox retorted. "Tell me, how do you think old Balladay keeps that Ike jacket from being absolutely riddled with burn holes? Is it made of some fiber like asbestos?"

Rock had no answer.

It did not take long before the dreaded grapevine rumor had become the authentic news of the day: Lieutenant-Colonel Jean Balladay had received his official appointment as the new permanent commanding officer of the 385th Quartermaster Battalion. All the officers had hoped that if AGRC put Balladay in charge at all, it would only be until they found a permanent replacement. Their disappointment was deep, and showed its effect immediately in a drop to an even lower level of morale for all the troops.

Rock's statement about Col. Balladay's lack of new ideas proved to be prophetic. Absolutely nothing changed for the better in the unit's function with this change of command. The same boring and non productive twice-a-day officer's meetings continued to demonstrate a total vacuum of aggressive leadership. Nothing happened to bring the unit onto a course to do its assigned, needed and difficult task of locating every one of the graves of the brave American service members who died in central France and needed the dignity of burial in official American military cemeteries or going home.

Thank God, Lt. Thomas' platoon continued to do a good job after they were detached from the group and freed from the hapless command unit. However, it could only do about one-fourth of the task assigned for the entire group. The 385th had already fallen hopelessly behind in its work, and it appeared to be poised to fall even further behind as a result of this change in leadership.

Balladay's appointment brought a definite change in the unit's leadership, all right, but much of the change came in the personality and ability of Col. Balladay himself. From the first day he took the reins of command, he was zombie-like. He had always had a tendency to yawn very often, but now he frequently napped at his desk, and even almost went to sleep in his beloved officers' meetings. Whereas he had always been bull headed and resisted change, an officer could now much more easily sway him to make almost any decision suggested, or to grant requests that were previously unthinkable. He was even slower than usual in making his command decisions—not that he had ever been quick and alert. He had acted drone-like since his first day of entry into the unit. Now, it was even worse.

It did not take the enterprising officers of the 385th much time to discern why their new leader had become such a zombie. Col. Balladay had become a self-appointed…shall we say…night watchman over his officers' conduct, and it had an unexpected ripple effect on a large percentage of his command. The colonel suffered from severe, chronic sleep deprivation.

Almost every night from about 10 p.m. until 2 a.m., one could find the colonel perched on a high stool in a small anteroom adjoining the hotel lobby, peering through the one-way-glass in its door. From this vantage point, he could observe all of the activities in the hotel lobby. Without anyone seeing him, he could, and he did, carefully observe any person who ascended or descended the stairways to the lobby. It seemed Col. Balladay had a fear some of the fine officers under his command might make an effort to smuggle women into their rooms and it became his beholden duty to prevent such shameful conduct.

His actions forced the officers of the unit to band together and create a secret roster of special "counter-watchmen." They selected and distributed a new code word for each day to keep one another informed of when the Colonel was present in the anteroom. As an officer and his date entered the lobby of the hotel that housed the officers of the unit, the late-arriving member of the 385th might ask the person assigned to lookout duty for that night, "Is the chicken on his roost?"

"You ain't just whistling Dixie," became one of the replies in the secret code for use if Col. Balladay were in his security guard's position.

Knowledge of Col. Balladay's nocturnal prowling caused a radical change in the night time habits of his troops. Whereas the tendency before had been to go to a nightclub, stay until it closed and come home. Now the tendency became to go to that nightclub, stay until it closed, then ply the orchestra with money and drinks to come home with them so the party could continue in their hotel's dining room until Col. Balladay went to bed. Night after night partying would continue until the lookout announced, "The chicken has flown the coop." Then the parade up the stairs began.

Rock had his girl friends, too, but he did not share the ulterior motives of many of his fellow officers. One of his purely platonic relationships existed with Robina, the receptionist and telephone operator at the hotel where the officers stayed.

Robina had possibly the most beautiful complexion the redhead had ever seen. Her dirty-blonde hair always appeared neat but somewhat utilitarian. She had a few more pounds of weight than most folks would deem to be advisable, and her rounded face seemed to match her abdomen, also rounded by the five months pregnancy it contained. She had married an Infantry sergeant who had returned to New Jersey on his release from the service, and she rather impatiently waited for her permit to join her husband. Robina shared every letter with her newfound, redheaded friend who was also lonely. Besides the many hours they spent talking as she worked in the evening and watched the antics in the lobby, the two frequently took short walks by the riverside and talked about life in America. These times together were mutually beneficial to Robina and Rock, and the two never became involved in any type intimacy beyond a friendly hug.

When Celia came on the scene, it was a different matter. Her looks were stunning and she moved with alluring grace and ease in any type of company. Her perfect posture served as her trademark, which seemed to be quite the opposite of most girls who were tall. Her always impeccably groomed, stylishly short blonde hair, and her flirty green eyes, healthy looking rosy cheeks and a winning smile were all parts of her aura that swept Rock off his feet. Celia had just entered her senior year as a pharmacy student at the local university. She spoke German very fluently. She also spoke English with the cutest accent the boy had ever heard, as well as speaking her native French. She had mastered the piano to the extent that she was considering a career as a concert pianist.

There were three things that continued to worry the boy about his latest flame. The first and least was her lack of despondency when her previous boy friend, Lt. O'Steen, left for discharge from the service. They had seemed so closely involved before that time. The second was the fluency of her German. He could not help but wonder if she had cozied up just as neatly with those Nazi types when they were the ones in charge of her country. His biggest problem was that Celia was Catholic.

Nevertheless, the boy was smitten. Their courtship grew quite hot and involved everything but sexual intimacy as the boy grew more and more certain of this being the one love of his life. Still, those lingering doubts remained in his mind.

The ten o'clock morning officers' meetings seemed to come awfully early for those party going officers and apparently for Col. Balladay as well. Stifled yawns and general stretching became the rule instead of the exception for most of them, in spite of many cups of GI coffee. Even Rock, a confirmed teetotaler and non party-goer, was affected in a strange way by this change in night time habits for the officers of the 385th. He joined with the others in the chorus of yawns.

"You guys are going to have to quit waking me up every night after midnight when you come in," Rock complained to Dan Wilcox as he turned over to go back to sleep. "You have waked me up and kept me up way too late every night for the past week or ten days. I'm still a growing boy and I really do need my beauty sleep," he continued in an irritated tone of voice. "I ain't coming down to sing with you drunks either tonight or any other night soon."

"I sure can't argue about your needing your beauty sleep, you ugly thing," Dan Wilcox said as he turned to leave. "Oh, by the way, Rock," Dan blurted out as he turned again to face the half-awakened redhead, "do you remember that Smits guy the MPs from the 419th picked up the other night for stealing a streetcar?"

"Yes, I remember him. How could anyone possibly forget anyone who was stupid enough to steal a streetcar?" Rock responded. "Why do you ask?"

"Well, old Col. Balladay has appointed me to be his defense counsel at his court martial, but PFC Smits exercised his right to choose his own counsel and he has requested that you join me in representing him."

"Me, a defense counsel?" said an incredulous Rock who had suddenly become quite wide-awake and tremendously agitated. "Why in this world would he ask for somebody like me to help defend him? Surely, he must know that I have never done anything like that before in my whole life. Why, I have never even so much as been on the inside of a courtroom when a trial was going on, and I have certainly never dreamed of representing anybody as a defense counsel.

"Me? Act like a lawyer..." Rock's voice trailed off in stunned disbelief.

"I suggest you take that up with PFC Smits," said Dan as he left the room to return to the party downstairs.

Rock hardly slept a wink that night as he mused about what he knew about PFC Smits and how he would tell PFC James Smits he could not help him. The soldier had hardly drawn a sober breath since he came to the 385th at its inception, though he actually seemed to be a quite capable person.

As best the redhead could remember, the scuttlebutt said that on the night in question, Smits had stayed a little too late in his bar haunts and had barely missed the last streetcar going to camp. He started the 12-mile walk back to the camp just a little after midnight. As he passed the streetcar-barn for the Lyon Transportation Company, Smits noticed a streetcar sitting there with its motor running. There was no conductor in place, so he boarded the streetcar and took off. He had only gone a couple of miles when the MPs arrested him and charged him with stealing the streetcar.

The young lieutenant could hardly sit through the 10 a.m. officers meeting that day. He pondered his newest challenge as a possible co-defense counsel and looked forward to his first meeting with Smits. He could not help but wonder what could he possibly do to help that soldier and why the soldier had requested him to act as one of his counsels. How could he tell Smits to get someone else to defend him? He was so engrossed in these thoughts that he hardly even noticed how boring that particular meeting was. Just as soon as the meeting was over, he hurried to the guardhouse to confer with PFC Smits.

"How in the world did you get yourself into a mess like this?" Rock inquired of his potential client.

"First of all, Lieutenant Notleks," responded Smits, "I want to thank you for coming to talk to me. I hope you'll agree to help me and I want you to know I have not always been a trouble maker. In fact, a year ago, I was a First Sergeant and I was expecting to become a Master Sergeant soon. Then, I got this Dear John letter from my old lady telling me she had run off with another man. Then my mother told me in one of her letters, that my sorry ex had been laying up drunk with this draft-dodger most of the time.

"I wasn't too worried about my wife. There are just too many other women in this world to worry about one. What has me so worried is that we have a five-year-old daughter that Mama tells me my wife is just shoving from pillar to post. Nobody is really taking charge or taking care of my little girl, and she means more to me than anything or anybody else in this whole world.

"I tried to get the army to give me a hardship discharge and I tried for an emergency leave, but nothing worked. Then, I guess I just turned to the bottle in frustration. Being drunk is the only thing that helps me forget. I know that ain't no excuse, Lieutenant, but I feel so helpless.

"The first thing I knew, I was busted all the way down to PFC—but that didn't matter. The only time I could get my little girl off my mind was when I was totally soused, so I tried to stay that way all the time. I'm here to tell you, I did a pretty good job of staying drunk, and you see what happened."

"I'm beginning to understand a little," replied a sympathetic Rock. "But why in this world did you pick me to help defend you? You must know I'm not a lawyer and, as young as I am, I have never done anything similar to this even once before."

"Yeah, I figured that, Lieutenant, but you seem to really care about your men, and you think a lot about things. I believe you even pray about 'em, too. I figure you'll find a way out of this mess for me," said Smits.

"I'm glad if I give that appearance and I do want to help you if your story checks out. However, there are officers in the 385ththat have done this before. Why don't you get one of them?" the redhead begged plaintively.

"Sir," Smits replied with a smile, "I've seen 'em all and I believe you're my man. I do hope you will help me."

"Right now, you've got me leaning that way," Rock replied, "but you never did answer my first question. How in the world did you get yourself into a mess like this?"

"Lieutenant," continued Smits, "I've been drunk too much of the time to really think straight here lately, but here in the guardhouse, all I can do all day long is think. I have really messed up this time, but I really and truly did not think of what I did as stealing a streetcar—I was just trying to borrow a ride back to camp."

"So you don't deny you took the streetcar?" questioned his new co-defense counsel.

"How can I deny it?" retorted Smits. "Four MPs pulled me off that thing and they are dead set and ready to testify against me at my court-martial. The worst thing, and the thing that really hurts, Lieutenant, is I could be eligible for discharge in four weeks if I hadn't messed up this way. Any hard time I have to do means it will be that much longer before I can see about my daughter. You've just got to find a way to help me, and I believe you're the man who can do it."

PFC Smits saluted a flattered and determined Rock who was now in a hurry to meet with his co-defense counsel, Lieutenant Dan Wilcox.

"Dan," asked Rock on their first meeting as co-counsels, "how in this world do you propose for us to defend PFC Smits at his court-martial?"

"'Lord, have mercy, as you rebels would say,'" responded Lieutenant Wilcox, "I don't see how we can come up with any reasonable defense for this situation. They caught him red-handed with the streetcar and four MPs are ready to testify against him. I thought we would just plead him guilty and throw him on the mercy of the court."

"Did he tell you the story about how his daughter is not being cared for and how he could get home earlier to look after her if he didn't have to serve any hard time?" continued Rock.

"Yes, but he should have thought about that before he stole the streetcar," came the reply. "These guys need to learn to take some responsibility for themselves."

"Well, he told me he didn't consider he was really stealing the trolley. In his thinking, he was just borrowing a ride back to camp. After all, he planned to leave it right on its track at the end of the line, didn't he? Is that really stealing?" Rock asked in a somewhat pleading tone.

Dan did not answer.

"Tell me, Dan," Rock droned on, "do you think you and I could ever really think the way lawyers think?"

"I really don't know," Lt. Wilcox responded in a pensive voice, "I've never tried and I'm not sure I can. Can you?"

"I'm not certain I can either," retorted a determined Rock, "but I'm sure going to try. I'm going to try hard for that little five-year-old girl who has lost both her father and mother. I don't really care that much about our client, PFC James Smits. He deserves whatever punishment he gets…but I do want that little girl to have at least one parent at home, no matter how sorry he is. Come on, Dan, let's get to work."

Together, Lt. Wilcox and Rock examined the case against their client. "It looks airtight to me," said Dan. "They have four MPs ready to testify against him and he admits he took the streetcar. What can we do but plead him guilty?"

"Aw, come on, Dan. Don't give up so darned easily. We're supposed to defend this guy, not quit on him. Now, let's look at the case against him and try to think like two lawyers. There has to be a weak link in their chain somewhere.

"Now, let's see…" pondered Rock, "their charge 'Theft by Taking' appears right on target, so we can't argue with them that much about it. Maybe we can prove what was in Smits' mind when he did this crazy thing. Even though he admits he took the streetcar, he didn't think of it as stealing.

"Old Col. Balladay appointed that snotty, pompous, brown-nosed, Major Tom Bradberry as the prosecutor. From the way that joker has been talking, I'm sure he thinks he has a lock on this case. Man, I sure would like for us to beat that conceited ass. Heck, Dan, I fully believe you are smarter in one day than he is in a whole week. In fact, in this case I believe the defense just might be one or two steps ahead of the prosecution in the department of counsel intelligence."

"But, then, there are the witnesses," objected Dan. "They have four guys who are professionals at it. We don't have even one witness who can really help us in a military court. PFC Smits with his tear-jerking story about needing to be home to care for his little girl might do us some good before a jury of women, but what good would that do before a military judge?"

"You may have a point there, Danny boy," said Rock as he continued to pore over the documents in front of him. "Hey, wait a minute. Look right here. I think we might have just found our answer," exclaimed Rock jubilantly as he pointed to the datasheet on the four MP witnesses.

"What do you have there, Rock?" Even Dan Wilcox showed a little excitement at the chance of beating Tom Bradberry

"It looks as if we have a veteran group of MPs here. They have been together in France for nearly a year, and one year is as long as the Army usually asks them to stay. Will you just look at that? Sergeant Pollard will be eligible to leave for home in just ten days; both Corporal Black and PFC Whitmore have only three more weeks to stay and PFC Romanowski will be eligible to go in just five weeks. If we can possibly succeed in putting off this court-martial for a measly 35 days, then there probably won't be any eye-witnesses against our client.

"I'll bet there is not a single one of those MP guys who will volunteer to stay just to testify against a fellow soldier in this trifling case. You mark my word, Dan. PFC Smits should be on his way home to look after his little girl in about six weeks, if we play our cards right."

"Well, I'll be damned, Rock, I believe you're right," a surprised Dan Wilcox exuded.

The counsel for the defense immediately began their delaying tactics in earnest. First, there was a request for more time to prepare their client's defense. JAG granted them two weeks for that purpose. In the meantime, Sergeant Pollard left for home and Rock began his countdown, "One down and three to go."

PFC Smits then went on sick-call because of intense shaking of his entire body. Dr. Schmedley put him on sedation and gave him a statement of disability for 10 days. His diagnosis was impending DTs caused by the sudden forced withdrawal from alcohol while PFC Smits was in jail. By now, Corporal Black and PFC Whitmore were safely stateside. "Three down and one to go," the countdown continued.

The Army did not hold court on the weekends and there were some fortunate scheduling difficulty by the military court itself. Add a one-day delay of the trial by a migraine headache for Lieutenant Dan Wilcox thrown in to boot, it was exactly 37days before a Lieutenant-Colonel Stacey Johnson of the Judge Advocate-General Corps, acting as the trial judge, pounded his gavel to open "The Case of the United States Army against Private First Class James M. Smits, Jr." By this time, there appeared not one single eyewitness in the court to testify against the defendant.

"You may call your witnesses, Mr. Prosecuting Attorney," said the judge to Major Bradberry.

"Sir, I have here four sworn affidavits from the MPs who handled this case," stammered a red-faced and flustered Major Bradberry as he faced the court. "PFC Smits' defense counsel has succeeded in postponing this court martial until all of the prosecution witnesses have been sent home—but I assure you, Sir, I have proof of the prosecution's charges right here in these sworn affidavits..."

"Major," interrupted the Judge, "may I remind you that the defense counsel cannot possibly cross-examine a sworn affidavit and that every American has a constitutionally protected right to face his accuser. Unless you can set some prosecution witnesses before me, this case is dismissed.

Then the judge added, "Furthermore, I note that PFC Smits is about 10 days past due for his normal time for discharge from the armed forces, and I order you, Major Bradberry, to see that his discharge happens as expeditiously as is possible. This man deserves to be at home."

"Yes, Sir," exploded an obviously angry Major Bradberry as he saluted and left the courtroom with the exonerated PFC Smits. He began the discharge process and PFC Smits was on his way home in only three days.

"And the beauty of it all, Rock, was that we didn't even have to say one word in that courtroom," said Dan Wilcox. He made no effort to suppress the grin that spread from ear to ear.

"Oh no, Dan, the beauty of it all to me came when I saw old Bradberry's face. He looked so mad…like he was about to spit out his false teeth, if those pearly white things in his mouth really are false," Rock said between ripples of laughter.

Before he had been in command for a month, Colonel Balladay had shown that his true colors were those of advanced senility. His leadership had become even more inept and ineffective because of this disability, compounded by chronic loss of sleep. Captain Schmedley, the group medical officer, began a second investigation into the mental capabilities of a commanding officer of the 385th.

It took Doctor Schmedley four weeks—four miserable weeks when the performance of the 385th was totally ineffective—to conclude his investigation with a report. Then it took another four weeks of the same type drudgery before the Medical Review Board finally agreed with Dr. Schmedley that Colonel Balladay was indeed a victim of a form of senile psychosis, and he should be retired from active duty.

To the great delight of a great majority of the troops; AGRC named Major Robert Thornton as his successor and he became the fourth commander of the group in less than six months. Thornton, in his late forties, was a very intelligent officer and had been responsible for most of the limited success of the 385th up to that point. On the unusual occasion when Col. Kilts or Col. Balladay had sought and followed the advice of Major Thornton, the 385th usually made progress.

Not a tall man, Thornton appeared a little dumpy. He featured a broad frame and small potbelly. He had receding, hair with reddish-brown tinge, and his nose loudly announced his prior excesses with alcohol. It was red, round and pitted in a manner that reminded Rock of W. C. Fields. His ready smile and quickness with a joke, or a belly laugh in response to a joke, made one relax in spite of the stern intensity in the Major's blue-green eyes as he peered over his half-glasses.

Major Thornton was a man of immediate and strong action who always seemed at least one jump ahead of everyone else in his thinking and planning. What appeared to be quick, on-the-spot decisions made by him had actually been reasoned out carefully beforehand, taking into consideration all the factors that seemed possible to exist.

His choice as the new commanding officer of the 385th was a popular one with both officers and enlisted personnel and the celebration began. The problem was that Major Thornton celebrated also. Spurred on by his supposed friend, Major Bradberry, Thornton broke his sobriety pledge and went on a drunk that lasted for two full weeks.

Rock always thought it was an intentional act on Major Bradberry's part to tempt Major Thornton with the fruit of the vine. After all, he coveted the job and he was next in line to take command of the group. In addition, he knew all about Thornton's weakness.

There was no second chance for Major Thornton. Someone immediately reported to the commanding General of the Twelfth Field Command of the AGRC about his drunken reaction to becoming commanding officer. Reprimand and dismissal from his newly assigned command were the immediate results for Major Thornton. Rock could never prove a thing, but he held the opinion that Major Bradberry was the one who reported the incident.

To make matters worse as far as Rock was concerned, Major Thomas Bradberry became the fifth commanding officer of the 385th Quartermaster Group. Bradberry was a product of the National Guard from the state of Missouri. He had apparently gained his original commission through some political connections his family held. Rock guessed he was fortyish, though he could easily have been older. His perfect posture made him appear to be taller than his actual height of five-feet-ten-inches. The Major tried to give the appearance of youth and self-assurance with his natty appearance and the swagger in his walk. He never appeared in any public place without his ornate riding-crop in his right hand.

His uniform always appeared impeccably cared for and he always used pomade to hold the perfectly straight part on the right side of his receding black hair in place. There seemed to be considerable debate among the troops as to what brand of hair dye the Major might be using.

His only prominent feature that persistently defied the major's careful grooming efforts was his big, black, bushy mustache. Each hair in the mustache seemed to go its own chosen direction, despite much wax and a large assortment of other grooming agents. Although he trimmed it and combed it faithfully and often, Bradberry's big mustache always looked as if it had been the loser in a cat fight.

Rock had little respect for Tom Bradberry…not one iota more than the Major's superior rank required. In the redhead's considered opinion (that a vast majority of other officers in the 385th shared) the major appeared to be an empty facade who would allow others to make most of the tough decisions. He then took credit for the good decisions while trying to shift the blame to others for those that failed to work out well. However, he did have to give the Major a little credit for a few small things.

"Well, Dan," the redhead said to Lt. Wilcox, "old Bradberry does see the futility of those two-a-day officer's meetings and he did have the common sense to cut them to weekly. I guess even a pompous old goat like him recognized that he could call special meetings any time he needed one, and for any reason."

"Yeah, Rock," replied Wilcox, "but the best thing he did was to cut out the girlie watch in the hotel lobby. I know that didn't bother your old Baptist butt, but it sure did throw a big monkey-wrench into some of my plans. It's a new day now, though. If you do your job well, you are okay with the major. He doesn't care about your private life."

Despite Rock's disappointment in the selection of a new commanding officer, he had to admit the effectiveness of the 385th was slightly improved. The unit began to make a little progress in its assigned tasks, even in those areas not covered by the platoon commanded by Lt. Thomas.

About this time, the unit had been in the field for six months and time for inspection of the 385th arrived. This brought a formal visit from Brigadier General Ted Collins, the Commanding General of the Twelfth Field Command, AGRC. Naturally, he found the performance of the group to be significantly deficient and far behind schedule. He informed Major Bradberry, "I want this outfit to be moved to its new assignment in Bad Tolz, Germany within the next 10 days."

Major Bradberry had never asked Rock for any type of advice before, and the redhead felt certain his CO detected the vibes of disrespect he emitted. The major appeared frantic as he entered Rock's room for the first time ever.

"Lt. Notleks," he said excitedly, "the General says we have to be out of here and on our way to Germany in just 10 days. You know we have already located about 20 bodies here that we have not yet been able to move and there is still a little area in our northeast sector where we have not completed our search. There is no way in the world we can do all that in just 10 days. What can I tell him?"

Rock experienced a feeling of great amusement that a 40-plus-year-old Major would ask advice from a Second Lieutenant who had not yet turned 20. His best effort failed to hide his grin as he made his reply.

"I don't know what you should tell him, Major Bradberry, but if it were me, I would say something like this to him. 'Sir, if you will relieve us of the responsibility for completing the search of the unfinished area in our northeast sector and for removing those 20 bodies or more we know are still in this area, we will move tomorrow if that is what you order us to do.'"

Rock could hardly believe what the distraught Major whimpered, "I can't tell him that, Notleks. You tell him." With that reply, the redhead's respect for his commanding officer fell several notches lower.

As he faced the General that afternoon, Rock was surprised at his own sense of calm while acting as aide-de-camp to Major Bradberry. After a snappy salute, he said to the General without any hesitation, "Sir, Major Bradberry tells me you want us out of here and on our way to Germany in only ten days."

"That is correct, Lieutenant," responded the General, "and what do you have to say on that subject?"

"Well, Sir," said a slightly less composed Rock, "you know a lot more than most people do about the history of the 385th. We have suffered through five different commanding officers in these six months, and the General removed some of them because they were terribly ineffective. Because of this, the morale of our unit has been quite low and, quite naturally, we have been low in our job performance. That is why we have fallen so far behind in our work.

"I am quite certain you are also aware of the facts in our current situation: that there are at least 20 bodies in the area that we have already located, but they have not yet been removed; and there is still a small area remaining in our northeast sector where we have not completed our search in its entirety.

"Sir," he continued with a gulp, "you are our commanding officer and we will do exactly as you tell us to do. However, Major Bradberry and I have discussed the matter thoroughly, and we feel it is impossible for us to complete this assignment within a 10-day time frame. We both feel that unless you give us a direct order to leave, we cannot go without completing the work you have assigned our unit to do. Along with your direct order to move, we believe we will also need you to release us from the responsibility for completing the search of our assigned area and for properly exhuming, identifying and giving proper burial to those bodies that have already been located.

"If you give us this direct order and a written release from any responsibility for work left undone, we could be on the way to Germany first thing in the morning."

"Well put, Lieutenant," said General Collins with a wry smile and a wink. "I can certainly understand why we have such a large problem here. How soon do you think you can be finished with this work and move on?"

"Sir," responded a much calmer Rock, "I have not discussed this time schedule with Major Bradberry. However, I believe if we split our work crews so we make two or three crews from one present crew and if we hire more temporary civilian help, we can be completed with our work and moved in about three weeks…four weeks at the most."

"I agree with Lieutenant Notleks," stammered Tom Bradberry as he wiped heavy perspiration from his brow.

"Then you have three weeks to complete your work here, and not one day more," announced General Collins as he rose from his seat in a gesture that the meeting was ended. "Major Bradberry, you start planning the move to Germany right away. I'm sure your Lieutenant here is competent to take charge of completing any and all of the other needed matters."

Although he still had no real respect for Major Bradberry and his competency as an officer, Rock had to admit that the Major at least did not stand in the way of those personnel who served under him as long as they did their work. After their extended session before General Collins, he granted the redhead, who had served as his spokesman in that trying situation, full freedom of action to finish the work in the field. The redhead had not expected such freedom even though the General had actually put him in charge.

The young Lieutenant relished being the boss of something for a change. He encouraged his troops and their hired civilian crews to meet General Collins' deadline for completing their work. "Each one of us has to spend at least one year over here away from our homes," he said, "and it would be nice to finally be able to feel some sense of pride and accomplishment in our work. Since we have no choice in the matter of where we are and what job we are assigned to, we might as well do the things well so we can feel good about ourselves."

The difference in attitude of the troops immediately turned almost 180 degrees. After six months of floundering in their fieldwork in France, the 385th finally began to function a little more smoothly, and in exactly 21 days, the men of the 385th had exhumed, identified and shipped all of the 20 bodies they had already located. In addition, they had completed the search of every square mile of their assigned area in France, with no further bodies found.

Rock's small detail accomplished almost as much in their last three weeks of work in central France as the entire Group had accomplished in six previous months, with the notable exception of the work done by Lieutenant Thomas' platoon. With the blessing of General Collins, they were ready to be on their way to a new assignment in Germany with their heads held higher than ever before.

The redhead allowed himself a small smile of self-assured satisfaction as he prepared to leave Lyon and his two girl friends there. He had been terrifically busy for the last three weeks and had not spent much time with either of the ladies. Now, he had only a matter of a few hours before he must be on the way to Germany. The redhead decided on a risky plan.

He would take both girls out at the same time, in spite of their jealousies about one another each had already expressed to him. After all, he would be gone tomorrow, and he had quite a few double entendres he could hardly wait to try in a situation such as this.

The trio strolled in animated and pleasant conversation down the walkways by the river, linked arm-in-arm, a redhead between two blonde types. When the evening ended with a kiss for and from each of the ladies, no feathers seemed ruffled, and the boy had an agreement to see each one soon.

He thought, *Mission accomplished*, as he packed his belongings for a transfer to Germany.

THE ROCK STILL ROLLS

Rock felt good about the whole world as he traveled in the small convoy heading towards Bad Tolz, Germany. From this new location, the 385th could cover the southern reaches of both Germany and Austria. In fact, Lt. Thomas' platoon had almost cleared one area in Austria, and they were getting ready to move into its Russian occupied zone. The boy could not help but think,

I'm glad that is not me. If the Russian Zone is the reward for good work, perhaps I ought not to try so hard.

And another irritating thought keep recurring in his mind as the convoy rolled along. His sense of pride and accomplishment withered as he thought; *here I am already 19 years old and supposed to be intelligent. It is foolish for a person like me to have to depend on someone who is usually a lot dumber than I am to drive me around. As soon as we set up our operation in Germany, my first order of business will be to get a driver's license.*

Another thought that kept recurring as the convoy rolled through the war-scarred countryside was that he would not take the attitude of a conquering party. He vowed to himself not to retain or to vent any of the hatred that his forced involvement, however small, in a long war with the Germans had produced. Their crushing defeat at the hands of Allied Forces and the destruction of many portions of their homeland seemed sufficient punishment without adding his own ill will to their already heavy burdens.

As the convoy stopped for a break, the boy decided to take a walk and stretch his legs. When he came face to face with the first German civilian he had met within that country's borders, he said a simple, "Good morning."

The old civilian apparently shared the same desire for friendship as did the young lieutenant. With an excessively deep bow, he responded courteously, "Oh, sie sprechen gut Deutsch." (You speak good German.)

Rock simply chuckled at the unexpected reply and decided to leave the matter alone. He breathed a small prayer that his every encounter with the German citizenry would be as pleasant as this first one had been.

When the convoy arrived in Bad Tolz, Rock quickly settled into his routine in the picturesque small village. He was pleased when he found that his assigned room overlooked the town square that featured typical Bavarian architecture that he had so often admired in pictures. There were not any signs of Allied bombing in this particular region, and no apparent damage to their simple infrastructure.

His bleak and bare office lay directly across the town square from his billet. That office would soon be bustling with business as German citizens reported American bodies buried in many different locations all across the countryside. However, first things must come first. Each day, in the redhead's mind, this matter of his driver's license loomed larger and larger. It became a pressing issue involving his self-respect and needed to be resolved right away. He must keep the promise he had made to himself as the convoy made its way into Germany. Rock headed for the motorpool and found its commanding officer, Lt. Mooney.

"Greg," the redhead asserted, "I want you to write out a driver's license for me."

As he filled in the blanks and signed the correct form, the more than cooperative motor pool commandant remarked, "Rock, it's about time you became a man. This paper will take care of you anywhere on this continent." He grinned as he handed the redhead his precious document.

"Now, I would like to check out a Jeep," said the redhead a little sheepishly.

"You'll have to see Sergeant Krantz about that," replied Greg Mooney with a half suppressed smirk. He apparently could envision the spectacle that was about to occur and had stuck out his own neck as far as he dared in this matter.

Sergeant Krantz did not hesitate to honor the request for a vehicle from his superior officer, but he apparently alerted every person in the motor pool area and all environs so that no one would miss the impending show. As Rock turned the key to start the engine, he felt as if every eye in the universe gazed directly on him.

Driven by sheer determination, he dismissed the strong urge to walk away from this task before he became too much of a fool in front of his uninvited audience. When he started the motor, he winced as it raced as if a schoolboy was at the wheel before he got the feel of how the accelerator should operate. Then, when he pushed in the clutch and moved the gearshift lever, there followed an agonizingly long grinding sound before he finally located first gear. The guffaws of the motor pool crew sounded louder than the noise of his racing motor and grinding gears; and the redness of the boy's face far exceeded that of his hair.

The young lieutenant's jerking, jumping, gear-grinding, motor-stalling exit from the motor pool area produced a wave of whistles, cheers and knee-slapping laughter of the type he thought was usually reserved for burlesque shows, and his face actually burned from intense blushing. He gave a wave of fake triumphancy to the gawking and snickering onlookers as he finally made a left turn from the motor pool driveway and pulled onto the highway. From there, he headed toward the most rural area in that part of Germany for a self-taught lesson in how to drive a Jeep. There, in the almost complete solitude of German back roads, the boy tried to simulate city driving conditions. He would stop on a hill and tell himself that another vehicle was only ten feet behind him so he could not allow his Jeep to roll backwards for fear of hitting someone else. He would imagine a car pulling in ahead of him, and test his reaction to that problem. He repeatedly imposed tests of this type on himself until he was able to handle each of these imagined situations with reasonable smoothness. For three or more hours, he continued this self-imposed driver's examination before he returned to his base.

Most of the motor pool crew had left for the day when his Jeep made a smooth right turn and came to a well-controlled stop at the motor pool's point for vehicle returns. From that point on, the redhead never again asked for a driver unless the vehicle he needed for his task happened to be one that his license to drive did not cover. He had finally fought and won that battle.

Now that he had the driver's license bug off his back, the young investigator could turn his full attention to his assigned work. Many American service men had met an unkind fate in this area, mostly in airplane crashes. It had now become Rock's duty to oversee the proper disinterment identification and care of the remains of some of them. The boy made a silent promise to do his best for them and their families.

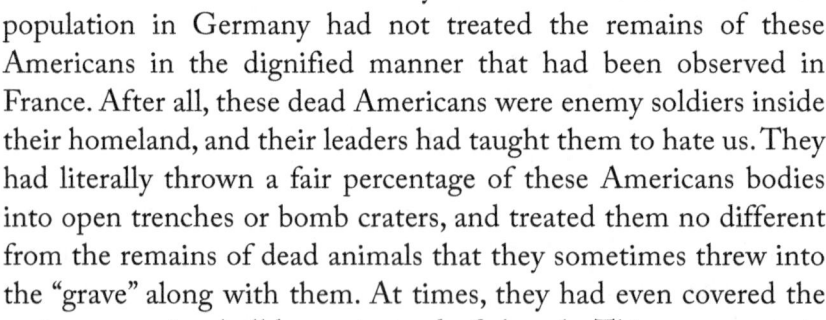

It soon became obvious to everyone involved that the civilian population in Germany had not treated the remains of these Americans in the dignified manner that had been observed in France. After all, these dead Americans were enemy soldiers inside their homeland, and their leaders had taught them to hate us. They had literally thrown a fair percentage of these Americans bodies into open trenches or bomb craters, and treated them no different from the remains of dead animals that they sometimes threw into the "grave" along with them. At times, they had even covered the entire area using bulldozers instead of shovels. This type scenario often called for the "skills" that special investigations officer, Lt. Notleks, had not yet completely developed.

The boy shuddered at the thought of such treatment of brave men. He did not relish the job of digging them up to give them a proper burial, but *somebody has to do it*, he reasoned as he set to the unpleasant task. *It is my assigned duty, and I would never think of shirking that. After all, I am a lot safer here than I would have been storming ashore on one of those islands of Japan.*

The new work in Germany had barely begun when Major Bradberry called Rock to his office. "Lt. Notleks," he began, "I have received a report from AGRC headquarters of an American Sergeant who was killed in the crash of a Royal Canadian aircraft in one of the small villages near our location."

"That really sounds strange, Sir," the young investigator responded. "There was really an American airman on a bombing mission in an RCAF plane? This is not some kind of sick joke, is it, Sir?"

"It is not a joke, Lieutenant. According to my report, this is exactly what happened," the Major responded. "It seems the sergeant's unit was stationed in England and he had been taken off flight status for some unknown reason, probably a medical one. He did not like not being in the action, so when he went on leave, he visited the RCAF unit. They had a bombing mission scheduled for take off that was short one crewmember of his MOS. The RCAF could not find anyone qualified to fill the spot, and our Sergeant Perkins did meet those needs, so he volunteered for the duty. The Germans shot their plane down over the target area, and killed five men in all. Four of them were Canadians and then there was our American, Sergeant Perkins. The local people buried all of them in one common casket near the village, according to my report. The village Burgermeister has all the dogtags in his office and he will give you whatever help you need "Lieutenant, I want you to bring that airman's remains back so we can give him a proper burial," the Major concluded.

"But what about the Canadians, Sir?" questioned an incredulous redhead.

"Lieutenant, you seem to be a student of the Bible. Doesn't it say somewhere in there something like, 'let the dead bury their dead?'"

said Major Bradberry as he rose from his chair. "That is a matter for the Canadians to deal with if and when they choose to do it. We must, and we will, take care of our own."

Rock felt a little more manly as he drove his own vehicle to the site of the five-man common grave. After his arrival on the scene, he struggled considerably over the daunting uncertainties of this most gruesome task—the hardest one of his lifetime. Trying to discover and identify the correct body parts of an American from among all those parts that the Germans had randomly thrown into a single wooden box without their dogtags would certainly be tough. The fact they had buried them in a swampy area more than two years earlier made it even more difficult. With a grimace, he began his ghoulish job. He found a skull with obvious GI dental work in its teeth and a pelvis with a GI belt attached. He found other bones that seemed to match these structures and labeled the body parts he selected as "Remains of Sergeant Perkins."

His grueling task completed, the boy felt uncertain of the accuracy of his work, but he consoled himself by saying, "I did the best I could do, given the situation I found myself in. If they had given me dental records, I could have been more certain. I hope Sergeant Perkins' family can get some peace now."

During the recent weeks in Germany, the redhead had spent much more time in actual fieldwork than in doing paper work as he carried out his job as special investigator. By spending much of this time working alongside the enlisted men of the 385th, he had developed a definite camaraderie with his cohorts. All of the troops knew that the Lieutenant drank no alcohol—was an absolute "teetotaler." Naturally, it became one of the stated aims of his enlisted personnel to get the redhead drunk. His men devised several schemes to try to attain that goal, only to meet with failure as the boy saw through their devilish devices.

Hoping to make his bond with his men even tighter, Rock decided one night while attending a dance that he would make his men think they had finally realized this dream. He took a single bottle of beer when one of the soldiers offered it to him, and guzzled it down in short order.

After he had consumed his beverage, the redhead made a pretense of being drunk and began to put on an uncharacteristic show. His men howled with glee as their Lieutenant chose another redhead to be his dancing partner, a chubby German girl whose head full of almost waist-length beautiful red hair seemed to be the only redeeming feature of her looks. Together, the couple took to the dance floor.

The problem was, the boy did not know how to dance. In fact, he had only been on a dance floor with a partner once or twice before, but that night he became a dancing demon, swinging his partner and swaying to the rhythm without missing a single dance for the entire evening. He continued to be much more interested in the cheering approval of his men than he would ever be in his dance floor technique or his dancing partner.

When the dance ended, the boy dutifully prepared to drive his dancing partner home. One of his friends, Lt. Roger Smith, pulled him aside with a request. "Rock," he said, "how about letting me take your girlfriend home tonight. I really like her looks, especially that long, red hair."

"That will be okay with me if it is with the young lady," replied the redhead who entertained no thought of either a long or a short-term relationship with the girl. He certainly had no plan for intimacy with her. When he informed her of Smitty's request, the girl was flattered and said she did not care who took her home. With that duty designated to Smitty, the boy ended his show of fake inebriation and went to bed.

The following morning before he received the enthusiastic reception from his troops, the young investigator felt somewhat sheepish after having made such a fool of himself the night before. The news that Smitty had been involved in an accident on the drive home the night before compounded this feeling. Word of their accident came as quite a surprise because Smitty had seemed in perfect control of all of his faculties when he left the dance with Rock's dancing partner. Otherwise, there would have been no such deal.

Rock quickly found Lt. Smith at the breakfast table and noticed a couple of bruises on his forehead, "What happened, Smitty? I hear you had a wreck on the way home. You didn't appear drunk when you left here. Did you go somewhere and drink more after I saw you?"

"Now, Rock, don't be so upset about nothing," growled Roger Smith in his most irritated tone of voice. "You are asking more questions at one time than I can answer in a single breath.

"The answer to your first question is, 'Yes'. We had an accident—a small one, mind you—and it was definitely not my fault. The answer to the second question is, 'No,' I certainly did not drink any more after I left you and I was definitely not drunk when the accident happened. The official report of the MP who worked the accident will confirm that. I'm certain you can look at his report if you want to.

"We were on our way to the girl's house and started around a curve, when I realized I had no control over the Jeep. The steering wheel just turned in my hands and the Jeep did not respond at all. I could not have been going more than 35 miles per hour when it happened. You didn't even ask if we were hurt or anything like that, but I'll tell you anyhow. Thankfully, neither one of us had any serious injuries except to that girl's pride.

"As soon as the Jeep came to a halt after a lot of bouncing and bumping, I looked over to see if she was okay. She had started screaming and crying and I thought she was badly hurt. When I got a flashlight to where I could see, there was that beautiful head of red hair lying in her lap. She was crying and trying to pull it back on. Thank God, she was only shaken up a little bit, but she was not badly hurt. The MPs were kind enough to take both of us home."

Smitty pounded his fist on the table and said, "You just wait until I see Greg Mooney at the Motor Pool. I'm going to really give him a piece of my mind for assigning me a Jeep with defective steering."

Rock's rookie status as a driver vanished in what was supposed to be a single day sortie into the British occupied zone of Austria. He was on a search mission of the area assigned to the 385th where there had been reports of gravesites of American service members in five different locations. He roared down a portion of the world-famous Autobahn at what, to the rollicking redhead at least, seemed to be supersonic speeds and thinking he had probably become almost a champion driver. After this exhilarating venture, he turned off onto one of the lesser roads that meandered through the picturesque countryside.

Since he had become his own driver, the boy was in a constant hurry whenever he was behind the steering wheel of his Jeep.

However, the old couple in the car ahead of him seemed to be in no hurry at all, and continued to hold up his progress on this particular mission. Rock fretted and fumed over his delay. Under his breath, he said some of those same words that had brought him trouble when he said them to Blackie in years gone by. However, there appeared to be no way to get around the leisurely moving automobile on the narrow, curving road.

Finally, there was a straight stretch of road with no oncoming traffic and the redhead pressed hard on the accelerator of his Jeep, sounded his horn and pulled into the left lane to pass the slowpoke. Just as he pulled alongside the other vehicle, it began a sudden left turn into his pathway. Rock's reaction was to slam on his brakes and steer his Jeep sharply to the left into the ditch, but the two vehicles had touched one another and wound up in the ditch together.

The elderly driver of the other car climbed out of his vehicle protesting loudly and pointing to his left-turn signal that was blinking. Rock could not understand a word of the old man's protest as he looked with amazement at the first turn signal he had ever seen. In Georgia, USA, all he had ever used or seen were hand signals. Rock felt positive that signal had not been blinking at the time he started to pass.

He tried to make certain that neither the old man nor his wife had any injuries and saw that the damage to their vehicle was very slight. He truly believed he was not at fault. He knew of no way to contact the authorities in this area controlled by British forces, so he simply got back into his vehicle and drove away as the old man still argued violently.

The redhead had traveled less than twenty miles from the site of his first incident when he met a large British military truck whose driver was driving on the left-hand side of the road apparently thinking he was still in London. He was bearing down on Rock's Jeep in a head-on fashion. As Rock abandoned the road and took to the ditch, his Jeep clipped a power pole. Fortunately for him, that particular pole was small and dry-rotted. It gave little resistance to his Jeep's bumper before it simply broke off and swung in the air still attached to its lines. It took all of the boy's newly acquired driving skills to control his Jeep and avoid turning over. The young lieutenant spent several minutes in calm and grateful meditation before he regained his composure enough to take to the road again.

A short while later, a logging truck that labored laggardly down the winding road blocked his hurried path once more. Rock impatiently looked for an opportunity to pass this vehicle also. The map he was following showed a fork in the road not far ahead and the boy hoped the truck would take the left fork, since he planned to take the one to the right. No such luck. The truck bore to its right with the Jeep doggedly on its tail when suddenly its driver, realizing he had taken a wrong turn, locked down his air brakes and the truck skidded to a halt. Rock thought his time had come but he was able to stop just short of rear-ending the load of logs.

Before the shaken rookie driver could put his Jeep in reverse, the log truck's driver, without bothering to look back, had begun backing up his vehicle. Its load of logs threatened menacingly to crash through the Jeep's windshield before Rock's frantic blowing of his horn finally got the truck driver's attention. By this time, the load of logs loomed over the hood of the Jeep and less than three feet away from the frightened boy's head. It was a terrifying moment that turned out to be harmless, and he again breathed a silent prayer of thanks.

After pulling around the log truck, the boy felt completely certain that nothing else could or would happen on this particular assignment and continued toward his small town destination. When he arrived at the central area of the town, he was surprised to find that the midtown intersection had five points and was quite congested. Visibility was extremely poor because the buildings were so close to the street, making a large sector of the main street completely blind to him. As he pulled cautiously into the intersection, a large truck roared out of this blind spot and literally scraped paint off the front bumper of his Jeep.

After four near misses on a single trip, a grateful but humbled young lieutenant conducted interviews that afternoon with the Burgermeister, police chief, volunteer fire chief and parish priest of the area to assess and confirm his information about American servicemen who might be buried in that area. Shaken and tired, the redhead began his journey back to his home base much later that afternoon than he had planned.

The brilliant colors of the setting sun almost caused the boy to forget his problems of that day as he eased to a required stop near the entrance to a British air force base. Tired and eager to get home, he eased his gearshift lever into first gear position, ready to speed off to the night of rest he felt he certainly deserved after this trying day. The Jeep refused to budge and its motor choked down when he let out the clutch. It rejected all his coaxing and use of expletives that he imagined had sometimes worked with Blackie. The gears were locked and the shift lever refused to budge from its first gear location. The redhead felt sick.

He had absolutely no knowledge of vehicle repair, so he saw no choice of action other than an appeal to his British allies for help. He walked to the entry gate of the air force base where the sentry on duty showed great surprise on seeing an American. "Hello there, Yank," he said excitedly. "What brings you here?"

"Well, what brought me here refuses to take me away from here. My Jeep is broken down right in the middle of the highway in front of your air base. Its gears have locked up and I can't get it out of first gear. When I let out the clutch to try to move, the motor chokes down."

"It sounds to me as if you do have a bit of a problem there, Lieutenant. Let me see if I can muster you up a bit of assistance from our motor pool," replied the British sentry as he disappeared to make the needed phone call.

After a few minutes, the motor pool commander appeared with his lead mechanic to try to give assistance to the stranded American. "Hello there, Yank. My name is Musburger. Welcome to our little world. What is your problem here?"

"Sir," Rock's response began "I…"

"As you Yanks say, 'Can that 'Sir" crap,'" the British Lieutenant interrupted with a little sound of rancor. "Just call me Geoffrey and let's forget about rank. Now tell me, what is the difficulty with your steed?"

"I'm glad to meet you Geoffrey. My name is Rock. I really don't know what the problem is," replied the redhead. "All I know is that when I wanted to move from the stop sign in front of your facility, I pushed in the clutch and shifted into low gear. When I let out the clutch to go again, the motor stalled and the Jeep refused to budge. It just sort of jerked a little and the motor choked down. I could not move my gearshift lever. I pushed in the clutch, restarted the motor, and tried to go several more times, but it did the same thing every time. It jerked a little and then, the motor died."

"Well. I must say, Yank, if you had to have a breakdown, you could not have picked a better place for it to happen than right here in front of our place. My grease-monkey here is a downright expert on these Jeeps and, if it can be fixed, he's just the one who can do it for you."

The Lieutenant turned to his mechanic, "Come along, Sergeant," he said, "The Yank is going to take us to have a peek at his unfortunate vehicle."

It took Sergeant Osteen less than one minute to reach his conclusion, "I'm sorry, Sir, but this is not a problem I can fix in a few moments. Your Jeep's transmission has locked up completely for some unknown reason. That will require us to do major repair work and means that we must pull it by wrecker into our garage. You will have to spend the night with us."

Rock squirmed uncomfortably. He had fully expected to be home for the night and had not prepared for an overnight stay. He had a number of things listed on his agenda to take care of on the following day, but they would have to wait. He could not walk to his base—and this had been a trying day. He wanted to go home.

"That's absolutely marvelous news," exuded Geoffrey. "You must tarry the night with us, but right now, we must hurry to arrive in the dining hall before everything is put away. They do close right at dusk, don't you know?"

Rock grabbed his briefcase from the Jeep and followed Geoffrey to the officer's dining hall where he was pleasantly welcomed by the entire staff. They made a special effort to feed him well despite the fact that it was past their normal serving hours. Rock responded to their efforts by answering tons of questions and enduring many backslapping greetings while he hungrily gulped down every bite of the almost tasteless food they placed before him. Geoffrey introduced the redhead to everyone who passed by, showing him off as if he were a special trophy. Their adulation both pleased and embarrassed the boy as they seemed to give him credit for all of the American efforts in the victories the two countries had shared during the long war. He knew well that he had done nothing more than have his Jeep break down in front of their base. Certainly, he did not feel that he was a hero.

When the boy had finished his meal, Geoffrey said, "Now, Yank, come with me. We're going to the Officer's Club."

"But I'm too dusty and dirty to go to a place like that. You know I've been driving all day and it has been a trying one," objected the young American.

"Oh, fiddle-faddle, Yank," Geoffrey brushed the boy's objections aside, "we're all in this boat together and war has always been a dirty game. You will be as presentable as anyone who will be there, and a day like yours calls for some refreshment. I know that our flyboys will wish to make your acquaintance. We rarely see Americans in this God-forsaken place."

The redhead reluctantly followed Geoffrey into the adjacent building that housed the Officer's Club. The attention of the crowd immediately focused on the red-faced young American and the British officers, who were well into their time of celebration by this hour, gave him a round of applause. Rock slunk into a seat and requested a Coke.

About this time, Captain Thomas Owens, a much decorated war veteran who was wearing the typical flyer's cap and silver pilot wings that were old enough to have their sharp edges worn round, approached the table.

"Welcome aboard, Yank," he announced loudly. "Most of us trained to fly our aircraft in your country and each time we would go into a pub and sit down, the waitress would bring us a drink. 'Won't you have a drink, sir?' she would say. 'Sure, and we'll have a drink. And where did this come from?' we would reply."

The Captain continued as his knees wobbled and he rested his arm heavily on Rock's shoulder to steady himself, "'From the management,' the server would say, and point to the bartender or the smiling owner. We would wave our thanks to our benefactor and proceed to imbibe our drink.

"Then, Yank," Tom Owens droned on, "no sooner would we be finished with that beverage when our server would be back with another one. 'And where did this come from?' we would inquire again, 'From the gentleman sitting at that table,' she would say, and we would thank him. Yank, that would go on all night and before we could leave that place, we would be falling-down drunk. So tonight, Yank, you're going to get falling-down drunk."

Rock's appeal that he did not drink any type of alcoholic beverage was completely ignored by his new and intoxicated friend. The boy felt forced by the persistence of his hosts and finally agreed to begin with a British beer. The taste and temperature of that warm drink caused him to remember the quote he had heard attributed to movie actress Mae West, who was reputed to have said, "As far as I'm concerned, you can pour that stuff back into the horse." He felt exactly the same way as he sipped slowly on the disgusting liquid.

After about half an hour of the boy's beer sipping, the veteran Captain realized his guest would never get falling-down drunk at the rate this was proceeding. He took away the beer and replaced it with Coke laced with Red Label Scotch whiskey. Rock's new strategy then changed to moving about the room and placing his drink glass beside an empty one every time he had a chance. He would then pick up the empty glass, but his new friend and self-appointed guardian for the night, Captain Owens, would soon replace that glass with a freshly filled one.

The redhead definitely liked the taste of the Coke-Scotch mixture, and he consumed a modest amount of the intoxicating beverage that night, although he could not exactly estimate the amount because of his glass switching. When he assisted their colleagues in putting three of the Brits, including Captain Owens, to bed about three AM, he thought to himself, *I can handle that stuff.*

Early the next morning, the boy reported to the air base motor pool and watched as the expert British mechanics disassembled the transmission of his Jeep. To the amazement of everyone, some previous mechanic had carelessly left a loose bolt in the transmission case. The bolt had finally enmeshed with the teeth of the gears and that was the reason for the locked-up transmission. No one could understand how this foreign object had not harmed the gears or why it made no detectable noise or how the Jeep had gotten that far with such a large foreign body enclosed in its transmission case. As the tired but grateful boy mounted the driver's seat and hurried back to his office at the 385th headquarters to file his field report, his thoughts were, *I hope I never have another day like yesterday. Sometimes, this driving is not as much fun as it was at first.*

About ten days after his return, Rock received an urgent summons to report to the Group Commander's office. Such summonses were common because of the incompetence of his commanding officer and the redhead had literally come to despise these meetings. Major Bradberry looked rather perplexed and a little angry as the redhead entered his door.

"You sent for me, Sir?" questioned the junior officer as he saluted the uniform of his senior officer, but not the man who wore it.

"Yes, Lieutenant, I sent for you," replied the Major. "We have a problem in our area of responsibility that needs special investigation. Apparently, Lieutenant Thomas missed one body buried in the area he just left. I find that hard to understand because he has always been so meticulous in his work. It is just not like him to do anything such as that."

"How did you find out he missed someone, Sir," questioned the redhead.

"By this notification I received from the office of General Collins at the Field Command Headquarters," replied the major as he handed a document to his special investigator. "It clearly states that a Sergeant William W. Brandes was killed as he parachuted over Tulves, Austria, and there is no such person listed in Lieutenant Thomas' report. I don't understand it. He is always so efficient."

"Well, it appears he missed this one, Sir, but did you notice that the grid coordinates on this dispatch do not match up with the coordinates on your map of Austria that shows the location of Tulves?" Rock questioned as he pointed to the map on the Major's wall.

Now, the boy became the one with the perplexed look. "Perhaps it's the Field Command office that has made an error and not Norm Thomas."

"That could possibly be the case, Lieutenant Notleks, but you can bet your bottom dollar I'm not going to be the one that tells them about any possible mistake they have made before we have proof positive it is true. That could make me look bad.

"The first thing in the morning, I want your Jeep to be saddled up and for you to be on your way to Tulves to find out exactly what went wrong, and how this soldier, this Sergeant Brandes, happened to be missed by the most respected officer in this entire outfit."

"Yes sir. I'll leave first thing in the morning," responded Rock with a salute, as he left Tom Bradberry's office to get ready for his trip.

The journey to Tulves was an uneventful three hours and the redhead arrived just as the Burgermeister unlocked his office. The official's apologies for lack of proper protocol in greeting such a distinguished guest were quite profuse. "Herr Lieutenant, please forgive. Die sekretarin is not here. How can I help? Your Lieutenant Thomas, he was here. He is goot man."

Rock would soon learn the Burgermeister had no helpful information, nor was there any more assistance to be found in the offices of the chief of police or that of the fire-chief. The lack of information gleaned from the usually reliable sources surprised and perplexed the boy. Finally, the aged local priest of the Catholic congregation in Tulves heard the full report from the young American investigator and appeared to fall into deep meditation.

"Now, let me see, Lieutenant. Just give me a minute to think here," he said in almost accentless English. "It seems to me…yes… I'm sure of it, Lieutenant, where is your map? I remember hearing as a young man that there used to be two towns known as Tulves in the country of Austria. The other town by this name was included in territory that was granted to Italy as reparations for Austria's damage to her in the First World War, but that war ended in 1919.

"Do you suppose by some stretch of the imagination it might be possible, Lieutenant, that your map has not been updated since 1919, and you may be looking for a town that is now in northern Italy?"

When Rock thought about such leaders as Colonels Kiltz and Balladay, he had to concede mentally that the priest's proposal was quite possible.

"Now let me see," pondered the aged cleric. "…Yes, Lieutenant, here it is on your map just south of the Austrian border near the Brenner Pass…and would you look at the grid coordinates…they match those on your map exactly. You would have found it if you had only gone by the grid coordinates on your map, but when they took you outside of Austria, you did not bother to look at any other sector. How did you Americans win the war with map information that you have not corrected since 1919?

"Lieutenant," said the old priest with the smirking grin on his face denoting his great sense of satisfaction, "your man is not located in Austria at all. You will find him in northern Italy."

The boy's head still seemed stuck to his pillow the next morning when, as he usually did, Dan Wilcox burst into his room. "Welcome home, Rocky Boy. I hope you had a good trip and have a report that will please the old man. He's been a bitch while you were gone.

"By the way, did you hear the news about our old buddy, Norm Thomas, and his platoon that we had working over in the Russian Occupied Zone?"

The boy was fully awake now. "No, Dan, you know well and good that I have been out of town working while you guys sit on your duffs in the office and gossip. But for goodness sake, please tell me about Norm and his boys. Are those guys being held as hostages or prisoners of war or something like that by those blasted Russians?"

"Oh, no, no, no, Rock. It's nothing as bad as that. I'm sure you remember when we talked about how unreasonable our wonderful "allies" were in allowing so few people to go into their zone to do the job and the unrealistically short time they gave them to complete their work…"

"Yes, Dan, I remember. But what in this world does that have to do with Norm and his boys? What happened to them," the redhead interrupted.

"Well, I'm also sure you knew that our diplomats were working with the Russians to try to get them to lessen the red tape and extend their deadline and make their chances of getting finished on time a little more likely," continued Dan Wilcox.

"Yes, Dan, yes, I knew all of that stuff. But, please, will you get on with the story?"

"Well, we thought they had everything worked out for an extension, but yesterday, while you were gone, the original contract expired. Those damned Russians showed up outside Norm's headquarters at six in the morning with tanks and truckloads of soldiers with submachine guns and even with aircraft circling overhead," Dan said, his face red with anger. "They made Norm load up and leave right then and they even escorted him to the border of their zone to see he didn't do anything else along the way. It may flare into an international incident."

"Why, those SOB's," exclaimed the boy as he fell back into his old speech pattern. "I wish we would go and get them right now. I would up for five more years just to see it, as badly as I want to go home."

"By the way, Dan," Rock looked questioningly at his visitor, "do you have any scuttlebutt as to what are the plans for finishing up Norm's work in the Russian Zone? Is he going to be let back in?"

"You've got me there, Rocky boy," Dan replied, "but there are some rumors that they might send someone from the unit in Vienna—just one man and a driver, mind you—to find all the bodies and then send in as many teams as are needed to remove all the bodies in just one day."

"Oh, my goodness, I sure am glad I'm not in that unit in Vienna. I cannot think of anything that could be worse than to be behind the iron curtain looking for the bodies of American service members right now when our relations are as bad as they are. I pity the guy who gets that assignment."

The boy quickly forgot about his conversation with Dan Wilcox as he breezed into the commander's office to give his report on Sgt. Brandes. He expected Major Bradberry simply to order him to file a detailed report with field command headquarters and this would end the matter. He had not counted on the huge ego of his commanding officer.

On hearing Rock's report, Tom Bradberry stroked his pride and joy, that impossible moustache, as if he were deeply involved in thought. "Hmm," he said. "It might make me look bad if we don't follow this situation through to its absolute end. You know, Lieutenant Notleks, we do not have a single graves registration unit in the country of Italy at the present time, nor is one planned to be there as far as I know.

"Our search of that entire country supposedly has already been completed, but I can imagine it's possible they might not have found the body of our Sergeant Brandes. It appears we have no choice but to search this matter out further so I can give a proper and complete report about that soldier to the Field Command headquarters."

Turning his attention to his investigator, he said, "Lieutenant, haven't you always had a burning desire in your heart to take a trip into romantic Italy?"

The major's feeble attempt at humor did not impress his lieutenant in the least, but the junior officer did recognize this situation as possibly being the opportunity for a very exciting adventure. He would have to cross both the German-Austrian and the Austrian-Italian borders and would need to drive across the entire country of Austria, mostly in their French occupied zone, to get there. There would be no place for him to find gasoline for his Jeep, so the trip would require a trailer and quite a few five-gallon GI cans of gasoline.

"Sir, if you think I am the man for the job and you order me to go, does it really matter whether I have dreamed of such a trip?" the redhead declared as he tried not to show his state of excitement.

"Your orders will be cut first thing in the morning and I want you to be gone from here at the earliest possible minute. I know you will have to get quite a few things together for this trip. Ordinarily, it might take you a day or so, but I want you ready as soon as they cut your orders. Get whatever supplies and equipment you need for such a trip and get them tonight. If you have a problem with getting anything you need, just let me know. I want that information tout schnell."

Rock located his map case and pulled out detailed road maps for the entire journey. Those maps showed the best roads to follow went south to Innsbruck, Austria, then down through the Brenner Pass into Italy. Just a few miles south of the Austrian-Italian border, the map showed what appeared to be a number one road leading off to the east and into a fair sized village located approximately 10 or 12 miles off the main highway. That should be easy, he thought as he continued to make his plans.

Although he did not smoke, he secured a few cartons of cigarettes thinking he might use them as bargaining chips if he needed some on his journey. He requisitioned plenty of C-rations and K-rations for his meals as well as an extra large number of chocolate bars and other candies "for the kids", of whom he was admittedly chief. He packed extra clothes for the cold weather he had heard about in the Alps.

Lt. Mooney, the commanding officer of the motor pool, assigned Rock his newest Jeep to use for this long journey and loaded a trailer with more than enough gasoline to make the entire trip. Though he had never before driven anything that pulled a trailer, he was cocky and confident he could do the job. Less than 15 hours after learning of his first long distance assignment alone, the redhead pulled into the Autobahn on his way to Tulves, Italy.

The weather was beautiful and the scenery exhilarating as the Jeep pulled across the border into Austria, then coursed alongside the Imst River for some distance before the town of Innsbruck came into view just as the sun was setting. The boy had never seen any place like it. Innsbruck was gorgeous. The picture-postcard appearance of this Bavarian town, which seemed to be hanging on the side of a mountain with snow-capped peaks soaring far above her tree line, almost took his breath. Why in this world did our government allow this place to be in the French occupied zone, he thought. A place like this could easily make a person forget about being homesick.

Once inside the city, the redhead found the American embassy where he was able to park his Jeep in a secure area to protect his precious cargo of gasoline. He then entered the embassy office to request a permit to cross the border into Italy. Inside that office, he met Jean-Pierre, a French army lieutenant attached to the American embassy as a special liaison officer. "Good afternoon, Monsieur Lieutenant," said the Frenchman in an unusually cheerful voice for that hour of the day. "What brings you to our fair city so late in the afternoon of this beautiful day?"

"I'm Lieutenant Notleks the special investigations officer from the 385th Quartermaster group based in Bad Tolz, Germany. My group is part of AGRC, the command that locates, identifies and removes the remains of deceased American Military personnel who have not had the dignity of proper burial in our regular military cemeteries in Europe. We have a report that they buried one of our good guys in or near Tulves, a little town located just across the border in northern Italy. When our unit searched that area, my report says they might have missed him. I am assigned to check it out, but I need a paper from you to get across the border."

"Of course, Lieutenant," Jean-Pierre replied in his very heavy French accent, "but you have come so late in the day. We were just before closing the doors…but perhaps that is a good thing. I can arrange a room for you in my hotel and you can join my girlfriend and me for dinner this evening. Perhaps she can also bring along her girl friend as a date for you. She is very cute and has a charming personality and she speaks almost perfect English. You will like her very much, I am sure."

"Oh, no, no, no," Rock insisted, "I have driven a long way and I am very tired. I do need a hotel room for tonight, but I do not want to butt into your dinner or to interfere with your date."

"But, Lieutenant," Jean-Pierre was adamant, "you do not understand. Her girl friend from Salsburg is visiting for a few days with my date and we were wondering what we could do to keep her from spoiling our evening together. You are like an answer to a prayer for me. You can solve my problem by taking this girl off my hands this evening. Then I will solve your problem first thing in the morning by getting your papers ready for your trip south. I will have your room arranged in the same hotel with me and we can check you into it after we get back from dinner."

The redhead did not like the idea of a blind date, but he did need to get his permit for crossing the border as soon as possible and he did need something to eat. Perhaps, he thought, he could make it work so that it would become a part of this adventure. "Okay, Jean-Pierre, you win," he finally acceded. "I will go to dinner with you and take your lady friend, but let me go first to the restroom and freshen up a little before we go. It has been along, dusty trip."

Crystal panned out to be just as Jean-Pierre had advertised her to be—her personality was charming, her appearance was cute. Her usage of the English language was almost perfect, and she exhibited a large vocabulary. The boy even enjoyed his rather bland dinner that Jean-Pierre ordered for him, and he ate the remains from Crystal's plate after he had gulped down every bite on his own. The evening was perfectly enjoyable and it fittingly capped an eventful, though long and tiring, day.

As the two couples entered the lobby of the hotel after dinner, Jean-Pierre tossed his new friend a key as he was disappearing with Katrina into his own hotel room, "You two are staying in room 14, right across the lobby," he said.

Rock was in an absolute state of shock. This was not at all in his plan for the night, and he really did not know how to handle the situation he found himself facing for the first time in his life. None of his training in high school ROTC, his OCS curriculum, or his Army training had covered this eventuality. Warily, he entered the room with Crystal and saw only one bed in the room and no sleeper sofa. He realized he had fallen stupidly and completely unaware into a trap that he should have foreseen. Now he had to make the best of the situation. He was tired and needed some rest so, after a short bit of conversation, the couple prepared for bed.

The boy could hardly believe he was actually in the bed with another human being who was not a member of his family, and was not of the same sex. However, her kisses seemed so sweet to his lips and the softness of her breasts so thrilling as he pulled her body close to his, the excitement was nearly overwhelming. As their bodies nestled against one another, the redhead confessed, "I've never done anything like this before. Have you?"

"Only once," she confided, "There was an American Sergeant stationed near my home. I dated him for a while. One night, he asked me to marry him and we did it that night. I never saw him again after that."

"Then it's not something you do all the time," he continued with a sense of relief. "In that case, I shouldn't do anything to you that would not be in your normal routine." With those words, he kissed her goodnight, snuggled close to her soft, warm, tempting body, and went to sleep.

The wake-up call seemed agonizingly early when it came the following morning. The redhead felt awkward as he dressed in the presence of Crystal, but his duty called. Their mutually respecting, tender goodbyes were said, and he was off to get his border crossing permit.

Jean-Pierre had not yet reported for work at the time when Rock arrived at the embassy office, and the redhead was glad fate spared him that confrontation. Another clerk quickly filled out the needed permit form for him to cross the border and sent him on his way. Before he mounted his trusted Jeep, he thoroughly checked his critical supply of gasoline. After finding that every can was present and full, he was soon gazing in awe and admiration at the gaudy Alpine scenery as he sped along on his way via the good highway that wound relentlessly through the Brenner Pass into the northern reaches of Italy.

As he made the left turn into the road that his map led him to think would bring him to Tulves, the boy felt confident of his map-reading ability. It was a good wide road with tar and gravel covering, but that good covering dissipated completely after approximately a mile. The road was still flat and had a large amount of gravel on it, so the driving was still relatively easy.

After only a couple of miles, he began to notice small rock fences on both sides of the road. These were formed by stones gathered from their fields and stacked one upon another by the local farmers. The road seemed to be becoming narrow and then narrower. Fear began to grip the boy as he worried about how his trailer was tracking in this cramped lane. It seemed to him he was in real danger of scraping the stone fences with both side of his vehicle at all times for the next several miles.

Rock shifted his Jeep into four-wheel drive, low range and low gear to begin the steep ascent up the Alps mountain toward Tulves. He winced every time he allowed himself to look at the sheer drop-off within three or four feet to his left and the equally-as-sheer ascent up the mountain on his right. Scared out of his wits, he thought, what fabulous drivers these folks must be to drive this road on a daily basis.

However, the situation got even worse when he came to a rickety bridge that spanned a drainage ditch designed to carry water under the road when it rained or when the snow melted on the mountain top. Rock could see that the water would plummet a hundred or more feet down the mountainside immediately after it cleared the bridge. He thought to himself, *so would I, if that bridge should give way.*

He dismounted from his vehicle to survey this situation and found the bridge to be made of sturdy timbers about six inches thick. It had what appeared to be good supporting beams underneath these timbers with two huge logs bolted lengthwise on top of this construction. He hoped these timbers left enough room to allow his Jeep wheels to pass through.

He thought to himself as he breathed a prayer: *Surely, I must be lost. The map clearly shows a good road leading all the way into a nice village and this is certainly not a good road nor do I see any sign of any sort of a village. Nevertheless, I have no choice except go ahead. I can not back up over what I have already driven across even if I knew how to back a trailer. God, help me if this bridge does not hold.*

Praying for his safety every second, he remounted his Jeep and forced its front wheels onto the edge of the bridge. Then he dismounted to survey the situation. The fit was so close that the long supports on each side of the bridge squeezed his tires so tightly they left a thin black film of rubber on both supports. Inch by inch he edged his vehicle across this obstacle and noted that his trailer wheel on the right actually mounted up on the bridge support at times. When his wheels were clear of the bridge, he breathed a deep sigh of relief and proceeded to force his vehicle further up the mountain. The next half mile was uneventful except for exhilarating views of the Alpine vista from so frighteningly close to a precipice that he hardly dared to look.

Suddenly, the road broke into a clearing and the grateful redhead could see three or four houses. He brought his Jeep to a halt in the first wide spot he had seen in a road since he left the Brenner Pass highway. A crowd of people surrounded him so quickly it seemed miraculous, gawking at him and speaking in a language he thought to be German. He understood none of their chatter and they did not understand his questions.

Finally, a tall, young, blonde-headed man with his face wreathed in smiles stepped out from the group and the boy heard a familiar, "Hello and welcome." Then the young man said, "My name is Cicero. How are you?"

"Uh…hello and thank you for that welcome. My name is Rock. I am very pleased to meet you and to know that someone here speaks English. Could you please tell me how to get to Tulves?" he asked in great frustration.

"Sir, you are here," responded the grinning Cicero.

His grin was interpreted by Rock as saying, *you stupid idiot, don't you even know where you are?*

From his present location, Rock could only see five houses and two barns. How could this tiny burg be the town shown so boldly on my map? This question still rang in his mind as a crowd of 40 or 50 people milled about and stared at him and his Jeep.

"Then, why are all of these people gawking so at me?" the bewildered lieutenant asked. "Do I look like a man from Mars…or is my tie crooked…or is it something else that I don't know?"

"Sir," an obviously admiring Cicero piped back, "do you realize you are the first person to ever drive a four-wheel motorized vehicle of any type into this town?"

The boy could not believe his ears. He knew the road had seemed treacherous, but never in his wildest dreams had he considered he might be a pioneer. Fear gripped his mind as he thought, *God, help me. There is no other road out of here and I have to travel the same one in the other direction if I am to get back home.*

Trying not to show his true feelings and to act business like, he said, "Cicero, can you tell me where I would find your Burgermeister's office?"

"Burgermeister?" laughed Cicero, "in this little hamlet? Don't make me laugh."

"Then what about a police station or fire station?" Rock implored. "I need to speak to the police chief or fire chief; someone who has a little authority."

"Not in our town. We take care of one another in this place. Our motto here seems to be 'One for all and all for one' just like the Three Musketeers used to say." A smug smile spread over Cicero's face as he gave his reply.

For the first time, the thought that he might be completely frustrated in this long and trying journey crossed the redhead's mind, but he continued hopefully, "Well, surely you have a parish priest in town."

"We have one, sir, but he's not in town at the present moment. Padre Jaucquine had to go to Innsbruck for some kind of meeting. He won't be back for at least two days." Cicero's smug smile progressed to a broad grin as he seemed to enjoy being the sole source of information for the American lieutenant, even though he was the bearer of disappointing tidings.

Rock tried to hide his keen sense of disappointment. "Then is there a place in town where I could get a room to stay for a couple of days while we wait for this Padre Jaucquine to return from his trip? I need to speak to him before I can complete my mission in Tulves."

"You can barely see the inn right across the valley there," responded Cicero as he pointed to a building that was only partly visible around the edge of the steep mountain cliff that jutted out into the valley.

Rock looked at the scene and surveyed the road he would have to travel to reach the inn. He decided it looked too risky to travel and thought he would walk to the inn. "Is there a place here that I can store my Jeep and trailer?"

"Why?" asked an incredulous Cicero. "The road to the inn is an excellent one compared to the one you have driven over to get here."

"I don't know about that. It looks very narrow to me and I'll bet there is a 70 or 80 degree slope on both sides of it. I don't worry about the up-slope on the right, it's the down-slope that worries me," the redhead responded. "I wouldn't even think about driving there pulling this trailer. Is there a place where I can store the trailer?"

A local farmer agreed to store the trailer in his barn, but he had no way to make Rock's treasure secure. Several men from the crowd helped the boy to loosen that valuable cargo from his Jeep and roll the trailer into the barn. "Sir, do not be worried about your gasoline. No one in this town would ever bother it," said Cicero with great emphasis.

I'm not really so certain about that, the boy thought without saying a word. *Jean-Pierre told me these folks made their living by smuggling things across the border. If they would smuggle things, then they might also steal them.* He said a prayer for the cargo he left stored in the barn and for his own safety as he began his short journey to the inn across the obviously difficult mountain road.

He had to pull his Jeep forward and then back up several times before he could make the 140 degree left turn into the road leading to the inn. Finally established on the narrow ribbon for goat carts, he found the first 200 yards or so were not difficult driving—but then he came to a huge rock vein that jutted out from the mountainside into the goat path. The valley below looked like a chasm to the boy and the rock sloped ominously to his left across the road, leaning toward that chasm. The boy examined the obstacle well and decided to continue on his course. However, when his wheels mounted the rock formation, they slid on that slippery slope and moved his Jeep several inches toward that almost sheer drop. With his heart in his throat and sweating profusely, he made it across that obstacle.

ROCK, Further Proof of God's Sense of Humor

After about another 100 yards of relatively easy but slow progress, he reached a turn to the right so sharp he could see no possible way to maneuver his Jeep around it. This left the boy with only the frightening prospect of backing his vehicle across the jutting rock that had nearly caused him to slide off the mountain while going forward. He did some serious praying in the time it took to travel those 300 yards in reverse, especially when he backed over the jutting rock that had caused him to slip as he had driven forward into the area. Finally, he was able to pull into the "main road." He breathed a sigh of relief as he moved his Jeep to the barn for safekeeping. Totally exhausted, he took his meager baggage and walked to the inn, where he secured a room to wait for Padre Jaucquine.

The boy thought the cuisine at the inn was an interesting change since it was just for two or three days, but he was quite thankful he did not have to eat it for a lifetime—and he would eat anything. All of the recipes were apparently of very ancient origin and based almost entirely on goat products, especially goat milk, cheese and meat. The scenery was a different matter—he could watch those Italian Alpine sunsets forever. He did his best not to rise early enough in the mornings to see the sunrise.

Padre Jaucquine's return came at the end of the second day as scheduled and he granted an appointment to the redhead for early the next morning. The priest opened the conversation. "Lieutenant Notleks," he said, "I hear you have caused some real excitement in our little hamlet. What is the occasion that brings you to see me and that made such a difficult drive become necessary?"

"First of all, Padre, I want to thank you for seeing me on such short notice—and, yes, my arrival in a Jeep did cause quite a stir, even though I never dreamed it was an unusual happening. My business here concerns an American airman, a Sergeant William W. Brandes,' began the special investigator. "I need…"

"Oh yes," the priest interrupted, "Sgt. Brandes. I remember him well. Poor boy, they shot him in mid air as he was parachuting to what he hoped would be safety. Those scoundrels…," the priest broke off. "I had a very nice funeral for him and we buried him quite honorably in the parish lot. We did the best we could for him with the Germans here and all.

"The Americans who came to get him did not think we had done anything wrong. Is there a problem now that caused you to make this long and difficult drive? Am I in trouble at this late date after all?" he asked expectantly.

"Absolutely not, Padre," the boy spoke in the most reassuring tone possible. "Please, sir, do not be upset. You did everything quite well and apparently with great dignity, and we Americans greatly appreciate your efforts. My country and the boys' parents are most grateful to you, Sir."

"Oh, thank God," Padre Jaucquine gasped in relief.

"Did I not hear you say, Padre, that the Americans came here and took him away with them?"

"Why, yes you did," responded the now smiling priest. "A group of twenty or more of them came and dug up his remains and put them in their own special casket-like box and took him down the mountain."

"But…I was told that no four wheel motorized vehicle had ever been driven into this place before I stumbled in here," Rock objected.

"That is quite true, my friend," Padre Jaucquine said gently. "The soldiers parked their vehicles at the foot of the mountain and gently carried him down on their shoulders. Three teams of soldiers and civilians did the work. One team did the excavation, another handled Sgt. Brandes remains and placed him in the casket, then the third group transported him down the mountain. It was quite an impressive ceremony, the gentle way they handled their fallen brother."

"Do you have any written records of their action?" the investigator instinct in Rock had to be sure.

"Only the cemetery record, but it is in a book and I cannot tamper with it." the priest said with a look of exasperation. "I will be glad to write you a ledger and sign it for your records, if that will satisfy your commander."

"If you could do that for me right away, sir, I would be most grateful. Then I could be on my way home before noon."

The boy packed his belongings quickly and secured the priest's report. He checked his gasoline supply once more and found it was as Cicero had promised—no one had dared to touch it. He could not say the same for his supply of chocolates and cigarettes. They were gone without a trace. He felt that was a small price to pay for his parking. As he mounted his Jeep, he breathed a fervent prayer for safety as he descended the mountain.

Rock's departure from Tulves drew as large a gathering as his arrival had brought. As he waved good-bye to the assembled group, Cicero and a girl friend flagged him to a halt. "My friend," he said, "Fraulein Eltsa and I wish to ride with you as far as the store in the village down under."

"What," Rock reacted with disbelief. "Do you know what you are asking? That is a very dangerous road and you might be hurt or, even worse, you could be killed."

"Sir, we have every confidence in your driving," responded Cicero as the couple took their seats in his vehicle. "If you could drive into this town, then we would trust you to drive us anywhere."

Flattered by their simplistic trust, Rock put the Jeep's transmission into four-wheel drive, low gear, low range. He did not touch the accelerator—only his brakes—as he gripped the steering wheel as tightly as any vise could hold for the entire trip down the mountain.

When Cicero and Eltsa thanked him for their adventurous ride, he responded, "No, I should thank you for your help and we should all thank God for a safe trip down the mountain." Then he hurried off to submit his report on Sergeant Brandes to Major Bradberry. Even he will look good to me after this ordeal, the boy thought as he sped down the highway toward his home base.

Major Bradberry seemed not to be very interested when his investigator reported that the body of Sergeant Brandes had been located, disinterred, positively identified and shipped off for proper burial. He had problems of his own. The Field Command Headquarters of AGRC had notified him that a full Colonel was en route to take command of the 385th and would arrive in very short order.

"Thank you for your good work, Lieutenant," he moaned, "but that is no longer the hot issue with me that it was when you left. Right now, the thing I have to worry about is what is going to happen to me."

Rock almost felt sorry for his commanding officer who had previously been so cocky. Then he thought, *I would probably be wasting my sympathy. I believe he already feels sorry enough for himself,* and he sought out his bunk for some much needed rest.

The new commanding officer, Colonel Frank Spriegel, came from a combat regiment that had an excellent war record. As the Army carried out a post war downsizing operation, they were eliminating his former command. However, Col. Spriegel's credentials were impressive, and the redhead liked the aggressive way he approached the problems facing the 385th in their field performance. Perhaps, he mused, the 385th will finally get on the right track.

Despite Col. Spriegels' best early efforts and modest successes in restructuring the group, it soon became obvious that the Field Command Headquarters was weary of the multiple failures of the 385th. It issued an order to disband the Group in its entirety. Rock's new assignment was to an AGRC Headquarters Group located in Vienna, Austria.

ONE MORE ROCK TO CLIMB

Rock could hardly contain his excitement as he and Dan Wilcox rolled into the city limits of Vienna. It hurt the boy deeply when he saw the damage done to parts of this treasured city by Allied bombs as they wrested control of the area from those hated Nazis. However, he knew in his heart we had to pay that price to free the area. Now, he thought, it's a shame that part of it is in the hands of those blasted Russians.

"Dan," he said, "this is one city I have always dreamed of visiting some day. During those early morning study hours while I was at Mercer, I listened on the radio to the Longine Symphonette playing all those Strauss waltzes and I dreamed about this place. It surely doesn't look like I pictured it."

"Aw, Rock, the only reason you like that kind of music is because you think those violins sound like the fiddles on that Grand Old Opry program you grit-and-turnip-green-eating Southerners listen to all the time. I'll bet you didn't listen to that classical stuff on Saturday nights when The Opry was on the radio." Lt. Wilcox could not resist getting one more jab at the redhead's southern roots.

"Well, at least it doesn't sound like your old Yankee polkas do. Every one of them sounds exactly alike. You hum one bar of any polka for me and I can tell you exactly what the next bar will sound like. You can't do that with Strauss or, for that matter, with Roy Acuff or Earnest Tubb," retorted the redhead as he brought his Jeep to a halt in front of the headquarters of his newly assigned outfit.

As he stepped out of his vehicle, Rock could hardly believe he was hearing the sordid sounds that were coming from the night club next door. He winced at the strains of the most raucous rendition of Saint Louis Blues he could ever imagine. The Dixieland swing style of the loud saxophone lead told him that the GI influence had swayed the tone of his beloved Viennese music and it would never be the same again. His disappointment was deep and lasting.

Brushing aside the momentary sadness of his introduction to the new music of Vienna, the boy said to Lt. Wilcox, "You know, Dan, I'm glad our time worked out to where we didn't come here two weeks ago."

"Why is that, Rock?" Dan questioned.

"Well, I figure that by now they have picked someone to go into that God-forsaken Russian-occupied location to take the place of Lt. Thomas' platoon. You told me those devilish Russians finally agreed to let us finish our work of locating the Americans buried there, but they will only allow one officer with an enlisted man as his driver to be there…"

"How in the world do they expect us to work when there will be only two men assigned to the entire area and they will be required to do the work that a whole platoon was not able to finish within their assigned time limit?" Dan interrupted the redhead.

"I pity the person who was picked for that job and given the duty of locating all the American graves in the entire area," Rock exclaimed.

"I'm glad we missed that, too," said Dan as the pair entered office building for their new headquarters.

"Welcome to the 432nd Headquarters, gentlemen," said Captain Freely, Adjutant for the group, as Dan Wilcox and Rock reported for duty. "Here are your billet assignments for your stay here. I do not have your work assignments at this time. There is a meeting of all officers here in the morning at 9 a.m. to decide on several items, and your duty assignments will probably come at that time. Sgt. Frix here will show you to your rooms. Get some rest from your trip, and I will see you right here at 9 in the a.m."

That night before he retired, the boy listened in awe to the tales of some of the veteran officers of the 432nd as they told about the poor relations with the Russian Army troops that occupied a sector of Vienna as well as a sector of the country of Austria. According to these officers, there were nightly confrontations between American and Russian troops who were off duty in the city. They also told him about an unofficial group known as "the Goon Squad." To some extent, the military Governor of Vienna directed this group, a collection of rowdy brawlers and drunken misfit soldiers who loved to fight. Every night, the Goon Squad went into the city to avenge what the Russians had done to American personnel the night before.

"If the Russians beat up an American corporal last night, then the Goon Squad will beat up a Russian corporal tonight. If the Russians killed an American sergeant last night, then a Russian of equal rank dies tonight. It is a dog-eat-dog world in this entire city and you must not let down your guard."

Rock felt a little uneasy being in this divided city as he retired to his room for the night. His room was located directly across from the nightclub and the loudness of the music greatly disturbed his rest. Probably more disturbing to the redhead than its loudness was the type of music he heard. Until the time when the nightclub closed and the music ceased in the wee hours of the morning, he heard only horns and drums, with some English words with a strong Austrian accent. There was not one note of the expected string music except for the rhythmic and loud plucking of the bass, and absolutely no Strauss waltzes. It was hard to take, but he finally went to sleep.

The boy reacted with total shock at the 9 a.m. meeting when Col. Freemond began the discussion by saying, "Gentlemen, the purpose of this meeting is to lay out our strategy for handling the bodies of our servicemen in the Russian occupied zone who have not been reclaimed by our forces. You are all aware of the heinous manner in which our supposed allies escorted Lt. Thomas and his men out of the area at a time when negotiators from both sides had almost reached agreement on a short extension for our people to complete their job.

"Most of you already know that, after much negotiation, the Russians have finally agreed to allow our group to have one officer, with an enlisted man as his driver, to come into their zone and search out the remaining bodies. A Russian officer of equal or greater rank than our officer will monitor our party very closely. We have agreed upon a date for the work to begin, and that comes day after tomorrow. No one has been chosen yet for this important, tough and somewhat risky assignment because we did not want to give our so-called allies the names of our assigned personnel in advance where they could have time to check up on him in any detail before he began his work. You know, they do have ways of finding out about people and we do not wish to help them in that process.

"There are eight officers in this room who meet the qualifications for doing this job. I have put the names of these eight officers on separate strips of paper in the basket in front of me and I will now ask our Adjutant to draw the name of the person who will represent his country in this important arena."

The boy felt as if his heart would jump out of his throat as the Adjutant reached into the basket, pulled out a folded strip of paper and handed it to Col. Freemond who then announced, "The name of the person who is assigned to this important duty is Second Lieutenant Selrach Notleks."

A mixture of elation and fear flooded the boy's mind because of the certainty of having a real adventure here and the unknowns in this assignment.

"Lieutenant Notleks, we will cut your orders early tomorrow a.m. and you will leave on Thursday for duty in Weiner Neustadt in the same location that Lieutenant Thomas platoon recently vacated so abruptly. Fellow officers, wish this young Lieutenant well in his new and important duty."

Rock was truly stunned. He had honestly expected this assignment to have already been made prior to his arrival, and he could not help but wonder if the so-called drawing had been rigged so that a newcomer would wind up in that ungodly place. At any rate, this undesirable job was now his official assignment, and he might as well make the best of it. He purposed quietly in his heart to do this job as best he could under the circumstances. Those Americans who had given their lives in a just cause deserved a decent burial, and his fear of those blasted Russians would never stand in the way of his efforts to provide it for them. He reported immediately to Col. Freemond's office to discuss the details.

"The rules you must follow are quite simple," explained the Colonel. "You will not leave your quarters unless you are accompanied by your official Russian escort except to return here to your headquarters. A courier will bring your meals to you daily from this headquarters, and pick up your reports. He will also bring any mail you receive and pick up any letters you write.

"The searching of each area will be the same as our usual routine has always been except you will not go from village to village and interview the officials of that area in search of information. You will only search the areas where we can show an American has been lost. When you locate one of our fallen comrades, you will lay out a detailed plan with clear and specific directions we can use to send the excavation party to the exact site on the date when we will exhume every one of the bodies you locate. We will have a separate team for every man. If you locate 50 bodies, we will have 50 teams.

"Sgt. Bazinoski will be your driver and your only American companion on this assignment. Good luck, Lieutenant. Be careful, but don't take any stuff from those bastards. Whatever happens, I will back you, if I have a chance."

He saluted the stunned redhead and left the room.

As Sgt. Bazinoski brought the Jeep to a halt at the international checkpoint where the two Americans entered the Russian occupied zone of Austria, Rock pulled out the travel documents for both men. Their border passes, printed in English, French, Russian and German, each bore a large red star seal from the Russian embassy affixed beside the Russian entries. It was not accidental that the redhead handed the passes upside down to the two angry-looking guards to see if these border personnel would turn them upright to read the information they contained. *A sly but rough test of the quality of these troops, who I would expect to be their best*, he thought with a wry smile.

One guard looked over the shoulder of the other who never turned either document upright as the two examined them. Broad smiles soon replaced the angry, questioning looks on their faces. The boy assumed it was because they identified the red star stamp on each pass. They then bent into the vehicle and embraced the two American occupants with bear hugs. "Camarade, Camarade," they exulted repeatedly.

"Camarade," Rock said half heartedly as he tried to recover from the effects of the body odor and halitosis emitted by the soldiers. That smell caused him to understand fully the old saying he had heard other GIs use, "I feel like the Russian army bivouacked in my mouth last night." He retrieved the passes and the pair soon pulled into the small town of Weiner Neustadt where they set up housekeeping in their new quarters, the basement of a partially bombed out school building.

Rock's smiling Russian "escort," Lt. Kasmakoff, spoke perfect English but brushed aside the boy's questions about where he had studied the language. He appeared to be only a little older than the redhead. His pale complexion, blonde hair and pleasant body aroma bore no resemblance to the bearded, dark-haired, tanned border guards from earlier in the day. His blue eyes could be penetrating, but seemed to sparkle as he laughed. He was trim and lithe and had a quite pleasant demeanor. Sgt. Bazinoski almost immediately gave his lieutenant a thumbs-up sign, and the trio was soon engaged in lively conversation. There was no hint of animosity of any type between the three who agreed to begin their mission early the following morning, a Friday.

The first day at work with Lt. Kasmakoff went perfectly. He had a list of the persons known to have been lost in the area that matched the list Rock had been given. With the aid of his perfect English and his authority, two American graves were located that day. The boy could not help but be pleased and to wonder if he had misjudged America's allies. At the end of the day, the team agreed not to work through the weekend, but to meet again on Monday.

"Well, Baz," commented the redhead, "this mission may not turn out so bad after all. It looks as if we have a winner in our Lt. Kasmakoff. If we make as much progress every day as we did today, we may be able to finish here in two weeks—three at the most."

"Yeah, Lieutenant, that could be possible," replied the Sergeant, "…But, somehow I wonder if he is not putting us on to try and milk some information from us. I'd watch him closely if I was in your shoes, and we'd both better be careful what we say in front of him."

"I know," Rock retorted. "When all is said and done, he is still a Russian."

Monday morning arrived and the Russian "escort" presented himself, but it was a far cry from Lt. Kasmakoff. The Russians had replaced Rock's new friend with another Russian officer, a Captain Ystrovich, and, as expected with the Russians, there was no explanation given for the change.

Captain Ystrovich was the prototype of Rock's idea of Russian army officers: stern and sullen, without a trace of a smile. He wore black boots and exhibited a tendency to click his heels together to show his authority. His dark hair and ruddy complexion, with the black stubble of a clean-shaven beard, caused Rock to think of him as one of the border guards who had gained the rank of captain and would see to it that no espionage was committed by this pair of American intruders. He spoke not one word of English.

The assignment had suddenly become everything he had feared it would be from the start; a dangerous mission of sheer drudgery with every possible obstacle put in place and the language barrier being a huge problem. To the boy, the new "escort" appeared to be much more like a prison guard, with the stature and temperament to match that profession.

When the courier from headquarters came that morning, he brought news that the Russians had closed the only road leading to the airport in Vienna, and of the general feeling among the troops that war hung imminently on the horizon. The redhead's quick mental assessment of his situation revealed many problems. He sat 35 miles behind enemy lines without a telephone, radio or newspaper at a time when war threatened, and he only had Sergeant Bazinoski to help him. The sudden change of escorts wiped out any prospect of an early end to his job, which now appeared much more difficult. Now, his only source of information and food supply, the headquarters courier, depended on the whims of the enemy for access through their territory. A feeling of fear suddenly gripped the boy, as he visualized that the 45-caliber pistol on his belt was his only equipment to assist in his possible escape back to the American zone if war became a reality.

Although he knew in his heart he would try to escape, his pistol could also ensure that he would not become the first prisoner of war of those blasted Russians. Rock had cause for alarm, and his situation called for three P's: prayer, patience and patriotism. He could do very well with the first and last P's, but that middle one of patience seemed to be very elusive for any redhead.

Since there was no refrigerator in their quarters, the pair had to depend on "C rations" or "K rations" for most of their food. In each of these meals, there was a packet of four cigarettes. Out of fear and frustration, Rock made an unwise choice and began to smoke these cigarettes to calm his jitters. It did not take long for him to become hooked on nicotine.

Captain Ystrovich proved to be every bit of the obstacle the American team had sensed he would be, and the quality of the interpreters assigned for the Russian and German languages as he interviewed his informants proved to be quite inferior to the abilities of Lt. Kasmakoff. Whereas the team had been able to pinpoint the location of two American graves in only one day with the Russian lieutenant, it took two to five days to locate a single grave while working with Captain Ystrovich. The captain questioned the motive and the process of everything the Americans requested, and when he needed to be away from the team at its worksite, he left an enlisted underling with a submachine gun to watch them. "I feel as if I'm already a prisoner of war," Baz confided to his lieutenant.

For about ten days, the tension that filled the atmosphere seemed so thick it was almost unbearable. The American team continued to pursue their search for bodies of their fallen soldiers quite aggressively, while the Russian captain seemed determined to frustrate and slow down their progress as much as possible, while he carried out his own duty of watching them for any sign of espionage.

Rock and Baz watched the captain equally as closely for any key that might bring about a change in his attitude. One day, Rock heard the captain speaking in very crude German as he attempted to ask a question of an Austrian citizen. The Austrian had no answer, so the boy answered Captain Ystrovich's question with his own crude version of German. The surprised captain showed the first trace of a smile the redhead had ever seen on that stern face. At last, they had found a crude means of communication. This seemed to light a spark of reconciliation from that time forward. The Russian captain seemed to lift his heavy boot ever so slightly and the two began a difficult process of trying to communicate in German, a language where neither possessed any degree of fluency.

As Captain Ystrovich slowly grasped the idea that the Americans were not spies and had no interest in anything except to complete their grave location assignment, he allowed them a little more freedom to move about. He quit leaving the guard with a Tommy gun pointed in their direction every time he had to leave for a few minutes. This relieved some of the mental strain and made their situation a little more bearable. It also brought about a small increase in the speed with which they could do their investigation.

Shortly after their "little cold war" had begun to thaw, a local city official guided the party to an American gravesite. He pointed to an unmarked location quite close to the grave and said, "You should not cross that line. That is the Austrian border with Yugoslavia. If you cross it and Marshal Tito's soldiers catch you in his country, you might face a firing squad,"

Captain Ystrovich and the rest of the party just laughed as they watched the impetuous redhead. He looked around in all directions to see if there was anybody visible across the border. Then, foolheartedly, he ran 50 or 60 feet across the line and, just as quickly, ran back. "Now I can truthfully say I have set my foot into Yugoslavia," he gloated.

The working relationship between the Russian captain and his redheaded American counterpart gradually warmed a little as their communication in the German language improved, but there remained a definite coolness. After all, the two countries were on the brink of war with one another. Rock had to be cautious about his actions to avoid any suggestion that he might be spying, while Captain Ystrovich did his duty and was quite watchful of the pair.

One Thursday as the trio, Baz, Ystrovich and Rock, walked down one of the main streets of Weiner Neustadt on their way to interview a police official, a male civilian bumped into the redhead with a tooth-shaking jolt. The boy had no doubt that such a jolt could not have been accidental and he reacted with clenched fists and red-faced anger—but the offending pedestrian walked rapidly away and melted into the crowd. Suddenly the boy realized: *That guy put something in my pocket.*

Rock could hardly contain his excitement. He felt certain that the underground had contacted him for some reason, but he knew he must not immediately pull out whatever his contact had deposited in his pocket for fear of his escort. He could tell by its feel that the object his intruder had thrust into his pocket was a note. That note seemed to almost burn a hole in his pocket for the rest of the working day as the boy resisted the urge to pull it out and read it. Finally, in the relative safety of his quarters that evening, he pulled the note that had been so abruptly and surprisingly delivered to him from his pocket. With trembling hands, he eagerly read its contents.

"Dear American Lieutenant," the note read in beautifully transcribed, perfect English, "Austrians for a Free Austria has noted with pleasure that you are present in our country. You are welcome here and we would like to have the pleasure of meeting with you and your Sergeant to have fellowship with you and to discuss your work in Austria.

"We know that you have the privilege of driving your Jeep back to your headquarters whenever it is needed, and you have not availed yourself of this privilege thus far. Our request for you is that on this next Tuesday evening at exactly six o'clock p.m., you would both get into your Jeep as if you were going to your headquarters in Vienna, but take careful steps to make certain you are not followed.

"Proceed on the normal route as if you would go to Vienna until you come to Third Strasse where you should make a right turn. Circle the block three times, always turning right. On the fourth time as you begin to go around the block, a garage door in the middle of the block on the right side of Third Strasse will open if we see no sign that the enemy is watching. You should drive into that garage so we can share some information with one another, and celebrate your coming to our area. If the garage door does not open, that will indicate there is a problem and we will contact you later for another meeting.

"Please burn this note after you have committed its content to memory, because it could bring death to one or more of us, and possibly to you, if it fell into the hands of the enemy. [Signed] Hans, Austrians for a Free Austria."

Sergeant Bazinoski's face lit up with excitement and amazement when Rock broke the news to his companion about his encounter with the underground and read the note aloud that the agent had passed to him.

"Damn, Lieutenant, I can't believe this is happening." He exclaimed. "This is just like one of those spy novels I've read in the past—only I'm one of the characters in this one. You don't suppose it could be some kind of a trap, do you?"

"Well, Baz," responded the young lieutenant, "you're not the only one who feels that way about this spy stuff. I have never dreamed of anything like this ever happening to me. And I certainly do hope it's not any kind of a trap, because I most assuredly do plan to go to that party."

"Me, too, Lieutenant, me too," Baz responded in his loudest voice as he broke into semi-hysterical laughter.

Rock and Sergeant Bazinoski loaded their Jeep as if to report to headquarters on the following Tuesday at 6:00 p.m. The boy's heart pounded wildly as he looked in every direction for signs they were being followed. Baz furtively turned their Jeep from the highway to Vienna onto Third Strasse at exactly 6:08 p.m. Both men tried to be thorough in scanning every nook and cranny of their surroundings and checking for any possible evidence that the enemy was watching or that they might be heading into a trap. The second and third times they went past the buildings on this Strasse still revealed no evidence of any unusual happenings, but their tensions mounted with each passage around the block.

Finally, on the fourth time around the block, a garage door opened in the third building on the right, just as their vehicle turned the corner. Baz quickly and deftly steered the Jeep through the narrow door and brought it to a smooth stop as the door closed quickly behind the two Americans, who had no idea what to anticipate. They had placed themselves completely at the mercy of their hosts.

"Welcome, I am 'Flash,'" began their contact as he secured the garage door tightly. "Before you ask the question, my name is a code name and it came from your comic strip character, 'Flash Gordon,' who travels throughout the universe in space. I hope to be able to do that some day. But for now, follow me to the meeting,"

Baz and the boy followed their young guide down the basement stairs and across an empty room that appeared to have been a machine shop in times past. Their host opened a cleverly hidden door near the far corner of that shop area. That door opened into what Rock assumed to be a tunnel under the street. Flash led them through that tunnel and into another building, up two flights of stairs, through a corridor, up two more flights of stairs, through a hallway, down another flight of stairs.

"Why didn't you just blindfold us so we wouldn't know where we were," questioned the boy as he followed behind Flash.

"Oh, I am so sorry," Flash responded with a blush, "but we cannot be too careful in this business. You know how rudely your Russian captain treated you at first…Well, you are supposed to be their friends. We are their enemies. Our treatment is much worse. Our lives depend on our being careful."

After a confusing maze of stairways and corridors, Flash finally opened a door into a room where about twenty people were waiting. Every person in the room rose from his or her seat and clapped as the Americans entered the gathering. Baz and the boy were completely unprepared for such evidence of adulation. They just stood there with red faces wreathed in smiles, and perhaps a tear or two.

Introductions were rapid and mostly unremembered until Rock shook a hand and saw the vaguely remembered, serious but happy face of the young man who had bumped into him on the streets of Weiner Neustadt a few days before. "You must be Hans," said the redhead.

The young man flushed slightly and said, "Yes. How sharp of you to recognize me after so brief an encounter. That reminds me to be even more careful in the future that I am not so easily spotted."

"Hey, man," retorted the redhead. "You don't get nearly knocked on your butt by somebody and not remember their face. Give me a little credit."

"I am sorry if I hurt you in any way, but we thought it was the best way to get us together," said Hans.

"Oh, you didn't hurt me. It just made me mad for a second. I thought you did your job quite cleverly and I am sure that Captain Ystrovich never suspected a thing," laughed Rock.

"You and I must talk while the others begin the party," responded the now smiling underground group leader.

It did not take long for Hans to determine that Rock had brought no specific message for him from the American higher echelons and that Baz and the redhead were there strictly to locate the bodies of all Americans so they could be given decent burials. Both young men then turned to the party in honor of the Americans—and what a party it became.

When the party broke up about 2 a.m., there was a period of heart warming goodbyes. Baz was in no condition to drive. Consequently, the redhead slipped under the steering wheel of the Jeep for the trip back to their quarters. The trip proceeded without incident until the Americans were within two kilometers of their quarters and a Russian guard with a Tommy gun stepped from his guardhouse and into the light shining above the street about 300 yards ahead of their vehicle.

The boy almost froze with fright because he knew they were not supposed to be out at this hour of the night or to be in the condition Baz was in at this very moment. He succumbed to his knee-jerk reaction. "Hold on, Baz," he said as he shifted his Jeep into second gear and pressed the accelerator to the floor scratching gravel from the dirt road. "We're not going to stop for that joker."

Rock crouched over the steering wheel as low as he could get, expecting a hail of bullets at any moment. As he sped closer to the guard station, his headlights revealed an Austrian pedestrian the Russian sentry had stepped out to challenge. On seeing him, the redhead breathed a huge sigh of relief, and hurried back to their quarters.

"Baz, only the guys who do our laundry will ever know how scared I was when I saw that guy with the Tommy gun step out toward our Jeep," the redhead said to his driver next morning as they arose to go to work.

It took seven weeks of intensive work under difficult circumstances before the American duo had located all of the graves that the AGRC had listed on the paper they furnished them. Twenty-one bodies were involved, and they could have completed the job in two or three weeks were it not for the bureaucracy and red tape of the Red army. Captain Ystrovich had eventually tried to make things run a little smoother, but the demands of his superior officers tied his hands. "The Russian army is worse than ours with its red tape," Baz complained on several occasions.

To mark the last day of Baz and Rock's assignment in Weiner Neustadt, twenty-one different American teams entered the Russian occupied zone of Austria for the single day the Russians allowed them for the disinterment of all American bodies buried there. With the redhead and his Sergeant's coordination, the work came off without a hitch. Those valiant Americans were at last on their way to the dignified burial they so richly deserved, and Rock breathed a prayer on their behalf.

Baz and the redhead returned that night to Vienna with their hearts light and free. They had completed a difficult task and both men felt they had done the work quite well. The boy felt certain they would receive an official commendation from their superior officers for their efforts.

Rock was grinning from ear to ear when he gave his final report on their arrival at headquarters in Vienna, and he had good cause. Not only did his commander give him a verbal commendation for a job well done, but he and Baz had survived under the most adverse conditions. Furthermore, he only had a few days remaining before he would be eligible to go home for discharge. The only sad note at that time sounded when Sgt. Bazinoski reported back to the motor pool, and the intrepid pair no longer remained a team.

Rock had a good bit of time to spend doing whatever he chose during those days of light duty as he prepared to go home. Now was a time when he could call on the Red Cross girls he had met at the canteen during his earliest days in Vienna. One of the girls was also on her way home and they were holding a going-away party for her. They asked the redhead to join in the home-going festivities, and he was happy to join them.

He had grown much more comfortable around girls and more confident in the smoothness of his ability to string them on. During this party, one of the girls poured an eight-ounce glass about half full of bourbon and offered it to the boy. Buoyed by his lack of problems from his experience with alcoholic beverage at the British air base, and in an effort to show off to the girls, he guzzled down the drink.

About this time one of the girls suggested they take a ride into downtown Vienna. The boy led the group out to his Jeep and positioned himself under its steering wheel. As he wheeled into town with the wind in his face, he had a dizzy feeling and feared he would pass out. The trip was quite short, so he gripped the steering wheel firmly and braced himself. They reached their destination safely, but after that close call, the boy swore never to drive again with any amount of any form of alcohol in his body.

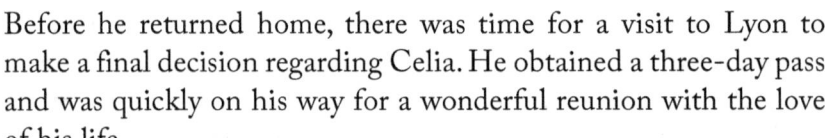

Before he returned home, there was time for a visit to Lyon to make a final decision regarding Celia. He obtained a three-day pass and was quickly on his way for a wonderful reunion with the love of his life.

Her hugs and kisses were as wonderful as he remembered them to be, and the redhead remained sure that Celia was the woman with whom he would spend the rest of his life. Yet there remained those nagging questions in the back of his mind: Why the lack of despondency when her previous boy friend, Lt. O'Steen, left for discharge from the service? What had been her relationship with the Germans who had occupied her country for such a long time? How and why did she learn to speak such fluent German? Could he put up with her holding on to her Catholicism?

His mind raced back to the time when he was 16 years old and a student at Mercer. Bill Rainwater, an older, married, ministerial student, had said to him, "Rock, you will soon be thinking of getting married. Let me give you a word of advice about that. When you go to take that step, don't marry the girl you want to marry."

The boy's mouth flew agape. "You're kidding me, Bill," he said in disbelief.

Bill continued, "No, I am not kidding. And I don't mean this in any ugly way at all, but you should marry the girl that, try as hard as you can, you cannot keep from marrying."

After that remembrance, the boy made a conscious decision not to take any drastic steps such as an engagement or marriage at that moment. He would wait until he got home and saw how he really felt about Celia after a period of absence from her. After all, he had made it without her for nearly six months while he was working in Germany and Austria…and he could always send for her.

In just a few days, he was on his way to Bremerhaven, Germany, for his return home. He hurried to board a Victory ship bound for New York. The ship was one of a myriad of small vessels the USA had built to help her gain victory in World War Two. They built them for service, and not for comfort. However, with the exception of a moderate North Atlantic storm that made many co-passengers seasick (but not him), his return home was uneventful.

The redhead reported to Camp Lee in Virginia to begin his processing for discharge from the service. The officer processing his discharge said to him, "If you will stay in the active service just 10 more days, you can be promoted to First Lieutenant in the Army Reserve."

Rock did not hesitate as he replied, "I would not stay in one more day if you promised to promote me to Major, but I would sign up for 10 more years if you would promise me we would immediately go after those Russian."

The boy was still steaming mad.

THE ROCK ROLLS THROUGH MED SCHOOL

When Rock arrived home after almost two years of Army service, several things had changed. He had saved virtually every dime of the salary he earned while he served his country, so he now had a small bank account to fall back on. He had grown from what he considered a sniveling baby into a man for whom he could have a degree of respect. Also, he had earned the right to participate in a wonderful program called the GI Bill of Rights. That program would pay a large portion of his education costs while he attended medical school, and would provide him with a small stipend to live on. It was an answer to his constant prayer.

Because he had been away from academics for two years, he planned to re enter Mercer University for a period of refresher post graduate work before he entered medical school. While he was in the Army, he had decided he wanted to enroll in the Emory University School of Medicine because only two physicians had really impressed him during his period of Army service, and both of them had graduated from that school. Prior to his being drafted into military service, he had been very quickly accepted at Emory and at the Medical College of Georgia, so he assumed there would be no problem in his being accepted again.

He could not have been more wrong. Nevertheless, based on this false assumption, he only submitted an application for admission to Emory.

He had planned to, as soon as he got home, date a girl he had admired but had never dated while they were in high school. However, she announced her engagement to a high school classmate on the very weekend the boy arrived. Since he had never dated her, he took the news in stride and decided to play the field for a while. Besides, Celia was still waiting in the wings. He was in no hurry.

After having seen so much activity in the Army, the boy grew restless as he waited through two full months for the winter quarter at Mercer to begin. On the day after Christmas, he attended a reception held for all college students who attended the East Point First Baptist Church and would be going to college in the winter quarter. At this reception, someone introduced the redhead to a rather tall and stately young lady who would be going back to Mercer in a few days. She was in her freshman year, whereas he would be a postgraduate student.

He liked Aron's posture and simple, colorful choice in clothing, and he thought her personality was quite pleasing. However, he was not impressed with her looks. He thought she had the largest nose he had ever seen on a girl. Nevertheless, after his enrollment in school, he decided he would have one date with her just to be nice to the hometown girl.

On this date, he wondered why he had been so unimpressed by her looks at their first meeting. Now he found her to be quite attractive with her greenish eyes, fair complexion and almost black, brown hair. Perhaps her nose was a little large, but he certainly had seen many that were much larger, including his own. Moreover, she possessed the prettiest leg she had ever seen on a woman and he found her personality to be completely engaging.

One thing that really impressed him about Aron was the respect she received from other girls on the campus. In his mind the boy reasoned, *a girl can fool all of us boys completely, but they absolutely do not fool one another. I believe this is truly one fine woman.* He found himself no longer thinking about Celia as he looked forward to the next date with Aron.

School became a total loss for the redhead as he wanted to spend most of this time with his new love. He began to monitor courses instead of taking them for credit, as he watched the mail daily for a letter of acceptance to Emory's medical school. Weeks and months passed and no acceptance came. Time became much more of a critical factor now, and the boy was genuinely worried because it was too late to apply to any other institution for the class beginning in 1947. In the meantime, some good things had happened for the key men who had written recommendations for him.

Emory required that at least one physician should write a recommendation for each applicant and, when the boy made his application, he did not know any doctor personally. His mother's gynecologist wrote a recommendation for him based solely on the family's reputation. Shortly after he wrote the recommendation, Emory had appointed that physician to its medical teaching staff.

His high school principal had also written a recommendation for him and, in the interim, that principal received appointment to the position of Superintendent of Fulton County Schools. His third recommendation had come from the dean of students at Mercer University, who many said was one of the 10 foremost psychologists in the United States.

Rock felt good about these references. Nevertheless, as time moved on, no acceptance came, and the time was getting shorter. A communication finally came from the admissions committee at Emory that his application was one of more than 1400 applications for the 65 places available in the freshman class of 1947. Panic set in and the boy redoubled his prayers concerning his future.

About this time, the head of the biology department at Mercer made a special trip before the Emory admissions committee on Rock's behalf and at his own behest. He informed the committee that Mercer had never sent them a medical school candidate who failed to receive an M.D. degree. He also said to the committee, "Mr. Notleks is our number one candidate for medical school admission at this time, and I believe he will make a wonderful doctor. I can see no reason for his not being accepted here immediately."

The boy was truly elated when Dr. Carver told him of his appearance before the admissions committee on his behalf. He was even more excited a few days later when a letter came confirming his acceptance as a medical student to be enrolled in the freshman class of 1947. He breathed a sigh of relief and a prayer of thanks.

The courtship with Aron continued with most evenings finding the couple together. One Sunday evening near the end of the spring quarter, they were walking hand-in-hand on a sidewalk in relative darkness. As they strolled leisurely past a group of houses where many of the married ministerial students lived, a friend named Alex was returning from preaching his Sunday night service. As Alex's vehicle swung left to turn into his driveway, his headlights highlighted the adoring couple. Alex stopped his car, rolled down his window and said, "Well, it looks as if I will have a job before long."

The trio shared a good laugh, but this episode apparently served as Rock's proposal to his sweetheart. From that time on, he and Aron began to talk about getting married. They were not able to make plans as to when it would occur because she still had more than two years to go in college, and the redhead had the full four years of medical school in his future. The distance between them as they continued their educations made marriage impractical at that time.

As Rock thought about his impending medical education, he purposed in his heart that he would make grades that were high enough so as not to make him conspicuous by low grades and yet he would make grades that were low enough to not be conspicuous by his high grades. He chuckled as he thought; *when the dean of the Medical School reads my name on that diploma I want him to say, "Notleks? Who in the devil is he? I never heard of him."*

A few weeks later, when the redhead actually matriculated into Emory Medical School's freshman class, he could not help but be concerned by the admonition of Dr. Steve Gray who looked over the top of his thick-lenses and sternly announced, "Look at the person to your right. Now look at the person to your left. Then think of yourself sitting between these two people. At the end of this academic year, one of you three will not be here.

"It is not the professor who will flunk you out," he continued… "You will be graded on a curve system in this institution and it is that SOB who is sitting next to you who will flunk you out."

With those discouraging words, Rock began to think about the situation and wonder which of those poor devils it would be. Almost two out of three of his classmates were Phi Beta Kappa's in college, and they were suddenly his competitors. He could almost feel a competitive wall of separation forming in the class, whereas there had seemed to be an early sense of unity among them during those first two days. Small cliques began to form immediately as competition to maintain a place in the class began.

It was quite difficult for him to study adequately and keep up with his courting at the same time, but he held his own with the biochemistry and gross anatomy, managing an A and a B respectively. Thankfully, the first quarter had barely begun when Aron made a decision to follow in the footsteps of her Aunt Mable. She changed her college major and began preparing for nursing school. This was exciting news to the boy because it meant she could enroll at Emory, and they could schedule their wedding at the end of that quarter.

Four days before Christmas, the couple became husband and wife. Married life certainly agreed with the redhead. He felt it was much easier to study when his life partner was nearby, even though there were constant financial worries. As much as the GI Bill helped, it was very difficult to squeeze Aron's tuition from the meager allotment given him for living expenses when he was already spending a large portion of that stipend for medical textbooks. Continuing to live at home in his old bedroom helped to keep expenses down, but the long hours spent in travel certainly cut into the time allotted for studying.

The couple was delighted when a trailer on the campus came open for them to rent…even though it had only 240 square feet of living space and had no bathroom facilities except for a community bath and shower building that stood fifty yards away and served the residents of about 20 trailers.

The excitement of trailer living had hardly worn off when Aron realized she was pregnant. This complicated matters quite seriously because of the already heavy financial strain. Rock was both elated because of the pregnancy and despondent about their financial situation. However, he felt that God had brought them this far and they would make it through this new crisis somehow.

When Aron's pregnancy reached the stage of almost four months, she had an onset of abnormal vaginal bleeding. Rock consulted her doctors and they prescribed bed rest. About two days later, she passed a small amount of tissue and some large blood clots. This was diagnosed as a spontaneous "miscarriage" and required hospitalization and surgery—a financial and emotional catastrophe for the young couple.

As Rock talked with the personnel in the business office at the hospital about the bill, he was told that a simple call from the dean of the medical school would result in a quite large discount on the hospital bill. The boy felt hesitant to make such a visit because he remembered his pledge to himself before he began medical school that he would keep a low profile with the dean. However, the financial situation demanded that he take this action immediately, so he made an appointment with the dean.

The redhead carefully explained his situation to the dean and requested that he call the business office of the hospital approving a discount for his student. He was quite disappointed with the dean's response and he made a pledge at this time never to darken the door of that office again. In a very unsympathetic fashion, the dean replied, "Notleks, you got yourself into this situation. Now get yourself out of it."

The couple paid the hospital bill in small increments over the next year, but the boy never forgot the interaction with the dean, and he kept his promise never to darken the door to that office again. He respected the dean's position, but held little regard for the man in that positions except for the fact that he was a physician.

As his freshman year of medical school drew to a close, the boy looked back with great satisfaction at the fact that he had learned so much during that relatively short period. He was doubly pleased with the fact that he had kept his pledge that his grades would be neither high nor low enough to attract attention. He had garnered the "A" in Biochemistry, but he did have a "C" in Microscopic Pathology. All of the rest of his grades were "B's." He had held his own with those Phi Beta Kappa guys…yet, he felt smugly inconspicuous.

Rock was excited about his summer job in the Biochemistry Department as well as his assignment to work with an associate professor in the Urology Department. Their goal was to develop a method to dissolve kidney stones in vivo by electrolysis. The boy developed a buffered solution of sodium citrate and citric acid that appeared to be harmless to the tissues of the kidney and served as a good electric conductor. At summer's end, the project stood at a point where he felt that if someone devised a dependable, expandable electrode to insert into the kidney pelvis, it might well become a feasible procedure in the future. He was grateful for the confidence his professors had exhibited in him.

The sophomore year brought its own problems, not the least of which was transportation to and from Grady Hospital from the Emory campus. The boy dug deeply into his meager savings and purchased a well used 1940 Ford two-door sedan. It was reasonably economical on gasoline, but it required constant addition to its oil supply. When he pulled into a service station, he would often say, only partly in jest, "Give me five gallons of oil, and check my gas."

Money remained a constant problem, and Rock still felt somewhat bitter because the government had excluded him from the V-12 program, which would have completely paid for his medical education. He had just begun his sophomore year when he learned the fate of those who had enlisted in the V-12 program at the time he had applied. Their support was complete for the first two years, and then the program was dropped abruptly because the war had ended.

When the boy heard this, he responded simply, "I would rather have half an apple that lasted to the end than to have a whole apple and it give out in the middle. I am glad to be where I am."

He managed a high B average throughout the very difficult sophomore year of academic study, but the beginning of his junior year quickly involved the boy in some of the practical things in medical school. He had drawn blood only once as a freshman, and that from a lab partner who had tremendous veins. As a sophomore, had "done surgery" on a stuffed sock—but never anything on a live patient.

On his very first evening of clinical duty at Grady Hospital, he was assigned to assist in the emergency room. Almost immediately, the intern asked him to draw a unit of blood from each of four black potential blood donors, the smallest of which he estimated would weigh 250 pounds. He did not dare to confess his total lack of experience, and accepted the task as a challenge. It buoyed his confidence when he was successful in obtaining units of blood from three of the prospective donors, and he felt somewhat vindicated when the intern was also unable to draw the fourth unit of blood.

A short while later, a person with a superficial laceration of his arm presented himself at the emergency room and the intern on duty asked the boy, "Notleks, can you handle that?"

The boy refused to admit he had never even seen a laceration repaired and impetuously said, "Of course I can."

After scrubbing and donning his surgical gloves, Rock draped the wound and injected the area with Novocain. He grasped the threaded needle in a needle holder, but his hand was shaking so badly, he could not put the needle in the proper position for suturing. Determined to do the job, he jammed his elbow firmly against his hip to steady his forearm. Then, by moving his pelvis in a dipping motion such as he had seen in some dance steps, he was able to do an acceptable job of suturing.

Despite his lack of previous experience, he successfully drew every one of 32 blood samples ordered on two surgical wards filled with desperately ill patients the following morning. This made him an instant expert in venipuncture in his own eyes and in those of the nurses on the ward.

Clinical medicine was even more thrilling and challenging than he had ever dreamed, especially with the famous Dr. Paul Beeson as the Chairman of the Department of Medicine. Even the taking of a medical history, thought by many to be so boring, reminded him of when he was playing detective as a child. One could gather clues to the diagnosis in such unexpected places, but history taking could also be quite boring, and facts could be elusive.

The boy learned a great lesson from an elderly heart patient when he asked him, "What medicines are you taking?"

The old man quickly rattled off a list of medicines that were familiar to the boy, but then he added almost as an afterthought, "And some 'dizzy tablets.'" In desperation, the young medical student searched for three days for the identity of the medication for dizziness while he waited for the family to bring the patients medicines. When they brought in his bottle of Digitalis, one of the oldest medicines in the pharmacopoeia, the boy gleaned a lesson he would never forget: *One must hear well exactly what his patient says. Then he must try to discern the exact meaning of what is said.*

Rock truly felt he had found his element as he entered the clinical portion of his medical education. His days in the Army "Ghoul School" and his field experience in Grave Registration had toughened him for the goriest incidents he might face. The time spent as a special investigator also lent valuable experience, and taught him principles he could now apply in trying to make a proper diagnosis of difficult diseases.

It did not take him long to recognize those physicians in the medical faculty who were the best teachers and were willing to "cast their pearls before swine" such as medical students. As he walked through the corridors of Grady Hospital and saw such a teacher on rounds, even if he did not belong with them, he would attach himself to that group if he had a free minute. It was on such an occasion that he gained another valuable insight when he heard a medical student presenting a case to Dr. Arthur J. Merrill.

The student introduced the patient by name and said, "She went to her LMD" (a somewhat cynical acronym for a local medical doctor, most of whom were held in derision by the academia) "who made the diagnosis of…ha, ha, ha…flu."

Dr. Merrill visually stiffened and turned slightly red in his face as he replied very sternly, "I did not."

Although Rock felt sorry for the student who had made this faux pas, he was glad he had not learned the lesson at his own expense. He made a mental note: *Always take a good enough history to know what physician has previously cared for a patient, and give that physician the benefit of the doubt before making any stern judgment of his abilities or his patient care.*

Rounds with Dr. Paul Beeson, the Chairman of the Department of Medicine, proved to be both stressful and richly rewarding. Although Dr. Beeson was quick to share his medical knowledge, he could instantly put any student on the spot with incisive questions. Moreover, his steely stare with those piercing gray-blue eyes was almost as incisive as his questions were. Nevertheless, the boy looked forward to those special learning occasions.

In his routine service rotation early in his junior year, the redhead moved to a surgical ward. His first assigned patient there was a critically ill, relatively young, black, male patient who had severe abdominal pain, high fever, a generalized rash that showed some evidence of bleeding into the skin, and a low white blood cell count. No one on the ward had been able to make a credible diagnosis on the patient whose condition continued to worsen. He had become an enigma to the surgeons and they had asked for a medical consultation.

On the rounds where the boy first met his new patient, both Dr. Beeson, the Chairman of the Department of Medicine, and Dr. Friedewald, the Chairman of the Department of Bacteriology, came to see the patient. They listened to the surgical resident's presentation of his patient's case history and went through every aspect of his medical record. Each of them examined the patient thoroughly. After much discussion, Dr. Friedewald concluded that they were dealing with the relatively new and exotic disease called Infectious Mononucleosis, which, he thought, had produced a skin rash in this case. On the other hand, Dr. Beeson contended that the patient was suffering from Typhoid Fever with rose spots, an ancient but quite rare condition.

Since it was his first day on this particular ward, the boy had not yet done the meticulous, all-inclusive history he needed to perform on each of his new patients. Immediately after completing the rounds with his highly respected professors, he undertook this task with little expectation of turning up anything significant. After all, the intern and a previously assigned medical student had already taken his history.

Nevertheless, the monotonous task droned on: Q. "Have you ever had chicken pox?"

A. "Yes." Q. "Have you ever had mumps?" A. "Yes."

Q. "Have you ever had German measles?" A. "Yes."

Q. "Have you ever had measles?" A. "No."

Considering that the patient had an unexplained rash and fever, this was a significant answer and the boy followed up with a question, "Have you been exposed to measles recently?"

When the patient answered this query with a "Yes," the boy proceeded to ask, "When did that occur?" His patient answered, "My little nephew had them about three weeks ago and I was with him at the time."

That is the exact incubation time it usually takes for Measles to erupt as a rash, Rock thought, and he became quite excited. Thinking he might be on the track of something significant, but ignorant of how it could be significant, the boy quickly turned to his copy of Cecil's Textbook of Medicine and went immediately to the section on

Measles. Here, he searched under the subheading of complications of Measles and found that acute appendicitis is a rare complication of this very common childhood illness.

He quickly shared this information with his surgical resident and entered a note on the patient's chart that in his opinion, the patient had acute appendicitis as a complication of measles, and that most likely the appendix had ruptured. The surgical resident concurred with that diagnosis and carried the patient to the operating room where they removed his ruptured appendix and, after a very stormy postoperative course, the patient recovered with no permanent damage.

Once again during his senior year, the boy transferred into a medical service and inherited a very obese, female patient who had the diagnosis of Cushing's syndrome. She had been on the ward for several days and had many studies done to determine the cause of her ailment. Shadows seen on her kidney X-rays appeared to indicate a mass in the adrenal area and the medical staff assumed she had an adrenal tumor producing her symptoms and signs. Dr. Beeson saw the patient on medical rounds and concurred with the diagnosis of Adrenal Cushing's Syndrome.

On his first glance at his new patient, the boy noted physical signs that led him to agree she did have Cushing's syndrome, but he saw something that made him feel quite uneasy about an adrenal tumor as the cause of her problem. This patient was cross-eyed so that each eye looked inward at her nose.

Rock knew that a tumor of the pituitary gland could cause both her Cushing's syndrome and her eye problems, so he quickly asked her, "Have you always been cross-eyed?"

Her immediate answer was, "No."

He quickly followed with a question, "Do you have any pictures at home that were taken at the time when you were not cross-eyed?"

Assured that she did have some pictures taken from that time, the boy requested that her family bring the pictures to the hospital as soon as possible because they might help in the diagnosis of her present condition. The surgeons already had scheduled her for surgery to have her adrenal tumor removed in just 48 hours. Although Rock expressed some doubt as to the cause for her Cushing's syndrome, he did not have enough evidence to back up his opinion if he entered a note into her record before the family brought those pictures to him. Naturally, the doubts of a senior medical student did not sway anyone's opinion after the Chairman of the Department of Medicine had stated his opinion, and the scheduled surgery was not changed.

The 48 hours passed and the family had not delivered any pictures. The patient died under induction anesthesia in the operating room. Shortly thereafter, the family appeared with the photographic proof that the onset of her crossed eyes had been relatively recent—evidence that strongly suggested her problem was in the pituitary gland. Rock immediately went to the patient's chart and entered a note giving his opinion that she had Pituitary gland induced Cushing's syndrome.

This did not help the patient at all, but it considerably buoyed the boy's confidence in his diagnostic abilities. Later, the autopsy showed a cancerous tumor of her pituitary gland for which no treatment existed at the time. Though saddened by the loss of his patient, he could not help but be exhilarated by the fact that he had noted a symptom missed by his highly respected professor of medicine, and it had led him to the correct diagnosis.

As the end of his senior year approached, Rock faced a financial problem for which he could see no solution. His G I Bill earned eligibility would expire in the last quarter and his savings account had been totally depleted. The only asset he and Aron possessed, besides their much abused, hand-me-down furniture, was that 11 year-old 1940 Ford with a hole in the floorboard. (The driver had to lift his feet when it ran through a mud puddle.) They had invested everything else in educations for the two of them. Moreover, no one in his or her family could lend him the money that might solve this problem, and the boy was quite worried.

A check with his Veterans Administration advisor showed that he did not have a problem. His advisor found that the boy's earned eligibility carried him exactly one day beyond the middle of his final quarter of schooling. He then turned in his manual and pointed out to the boy the regulation that if eligibility carried a student beyond the middle of a quarter or semester, benefits were payable for that entire period of study. With a sense of great relief, the redhead completed his final quarter of medical school. He took and passed the Georgia State Medical Board examination and accepted his M. D. degree.

EPILOGUE

As the trusty old 1940 Ford carried the new nurse-and-doctor couple to an internship in Shreveport, Louisiana, his last step in preparation for his missionary journey or medical practice, Rock turned to Aron and remarked, "It just dawned on me.

"Who ever heard of a man that was medically unfit to study medicine in the Navy, yet was physically qualified to potentially lead a platoon of soldiers in combat? I'll bet I'm the first. If it had not been for my meaningless deformity, I would have been in the Navy V-12 program which would have ended in my sophomore year, and I would not have been eligible for the GI Bill. Worse than that, we might have never met.

"I don't know how we could have possibly paid for those last two years of medical school out of our pockets when that program ended. Because of my deformity, I went to the army instead, and we had the exact number of days of GI Bill needed to complete my medical education. One day more would have been superfluous—one day less might have been critical. That deformity was put there when, as the Bible says, I was 'formed in my mother's womb.'

"Here I have this obvious miracle in my life, and who can I tell? Certainly I can't report it to the Women's Missionary Union. And they tell me God doesn't have a sense of humor."

www.ingramcontent.com/pod-product-compliance
Lightning Source LLC
LaVergne TN
LVHW011935070526
838202LV00054B/4651